The Great Arrogation:

Why America is Not a Party to the Battle of Armageddon

R.C. Caudill

First Edition Published by :

Seabury Press *2024*

seaburypress.online

Copyright © 2024 by R.C. Caudill

thegreatarrogation.com

First Edition

ISBN: 979-8-89379-129-7

Table of contents

ONE

Chapter 1: Introduction

Thirty four trillion dollars in debt, record homelessness, and division among the masses in nearly every aspect of life. America, the home of the free and the land of the brave, is hardly a shadow of what it once was just a few decades ago. The last decade has seen the nation spiral in a direction that is disturbing to any interested onlooker. What happened? Where did everything go wrong? Why is the once global symbol of democracy crumbling before our eyes?

This book ties the answer to these questions to an ancient question of Biblical origin. A crucial ally to Israel since its rebirth in 1948, as we now know it, America should, by all accounts, respond to aid the tiny Jewish nation during an invasion perpetrated by much larger aggressors. This scenario is described in Ezekiel 38 and 39. However, the once shining beacon of freedom will simply be unable or unwilling to respond. But why?

The Ezekiel 38 War, also known as the Final Battle or the Gog-Magog War, will be the final confrontation of the forces of light against those of darkness. Of course, the ultimate victory belongs to God. However, there are many considerations along the way.

This work will first look at the Ezekiel 38 War in greater detail and examine which nations will be present according to scripture. It will also show how the dark, cruel, yet carefully planned strategies of two socialist superpowers, China and Russia, discreetly impact the masses. Furthermore, their plan allows them to manipulate national and global events that have earth-shaking implications. It will also examine how those nations are acting in unison to arrogate the United States, which ultimately makes it unable to aid Israel during its greatest time of need.

Every major sign of the last days, as Jesus described them in Matthew, is visible to us daily. Artificial intelligence and the Hamas and Israeli war have further hastened the fulfillment of the end-time events. Meanwhile, division, demoralization, and record national and private debt are manifestations of China and Russia's success. Although the will of God will inevitably be carried out precisely as it should be, this book will explain what we can expect soon from a national, economic, and prophetic standpoint.

Special Thanks

I want to give thanks to God the Father for another day of my life and the ability to complete this work. Also, for giving his son Jesus Christ as a sacrifice for the sins of the world. Without him, nothing would be possible. I also want to thank my wonderful family for always believing in me and showing me the way. I will never depart from it.

T W O

Chapter 2: The Final War

I ntroduction

Ezekiel's book in the Bible contains a prophecy known as the Ezekiel 38 War, which has long intrigued and captivated the minds of Christians throughout centuries. This prophetic event, described in vivid detail, portrays a final battle involving various nations coming to plunder Israel. In this chapter, we explore the modern nations involved in the Ezekiel 38 War and compare them to their Biblical names. In addition, we will delve into the connection between the Final Battle of Ezekiel 38 and the Dead Sea Scrolls' War Scroll. Lastly, we will discuss popular Christian theories as to why the United States is not mentioned in this apocalyptic event.

The Ezekiel 38 War: A Biblical Perspective

The prophecy of the Ezekiel 38 War is found in the Book of Ezekiel in chapters 38 and 39. The war describes a coalition of nations that will gather against Israel in the last days for the Final Battle of the forces of good versus those of evil. Admittedly, the specific identification of these nations can be a matter of interpretation; they most certainly correspond to a group of modern nations and a very real war. Regardless, I want to underline that while the identification of these nations is not unanimously agreed upon across the board by believers due to different interpretations, a general conclusion is widely accepted as to their identity.

Modern Nations Compared with Their Biblical Names

We can identify the modern nations involved in the Ezekiel 38 War by referencing their Biblical names and using widely accepted translations put forward by Biblical and Hebrew scholars. One of the key nations mentioned in the prophecy is Magog. In the Bible, Magog is associated with Japheth's descendants, one of Noah's sons. Magog represents modern-day Central Asia, a string of nations that are now either part of Russia or are essentially controlled by it. The latter has not changed since the Soviet Union, as they all served as Soviet satellite states. Regarding Central Asia, it is important to note the genetic, cultural, and linguistic similarities between the region and Turkey.

The names of Japheth's, (the son of Noah (Genesis 10:2) sixth and fifth sons were Meshech and Tubal in Ezekiel 38:2-3. Additionally, Meshech and Tubal are mentioned in Ezekiel 27:13 as Tyre's (modern-day Lebanon) trading partners. Meshech and Tubal most likely relate to the ancient Moshi and Tubalu who lived in the region in Ezekiel's day, mainly south of the Black and Caspian Seas. These countries would now firmly be in what is now Turkey, and in portions of Northern Iran, Southern Russia, and the surrounding region. All of which are predominantly Muslim.

Rosh is used as the proper name for Ros in the Greek translation. Some believe this passage alludes to Russia as the "prince of Rosh" because the ancient Sarmations were known as the Ras, Rashu, and Rus and lived in Rasapu, which is now Southern Russia. Ezekiel 38 verses 6 and 15, which predicts that the invasion will come from far-flung regions of the north (and Russia is quite far), is another passage used to support the theory that Rosh is modern Russia. Further evidence comes from Moscow being directly north of Jerusalem.

The other nations mentioned in Ezekiel 38 include Persia, Cush, Put, Gomer, and Togarmah. Persia is commonly associated with modern-day Iran, while Cush and Put are believed to correspond to regions in Africa, namely Sudan and Libya, respectively. Gomer and Togarmah are associated with areas in modern Turkey and the surrounding areas.

It is important to approach these identifications with some caution, as the geopolitical landscape has changed over time, and the identification of ancient nations with modern counterparts can be complex. Nevertheless, these comparisons provide a framework for understanding the potential involvement of modern nations in the Ezekiel 38 War, and it can be safely concluded that a North African, Middle Eastern, and Central Asian coalition of nations led by Russia will come against Israel in the Final Battle, and there will be no allied nation to assist it.

Dead Sea Scrolls' War scrolls and the Final Battle of Ezekiel 38

The Dead Sea Scrolls, discovered in the mid-20th century, shed light on ancient Jewish texts and provide valuable insights into the beliefs and practices of the community that produced them. Among these scrolls is the War Scroll, which contains instructions for an eschatological war against the forces of evil.

Some scholars have drawn parallels between the Final Battle described in the Ezekiel 38 prophecy and the War Scroll. Both texts depict a climactic conflict between the righteous and the wicked, with divine intervention ensuring the victory of the righteous. While the specific details may differ, the overarching themes of a Final Battle and divine intervention are present in both texts. The Dead Sea Scrolls were written before Jesus's time and the New Testament. Therefore, any connections between the War Scroll and the Final Battle of Ezekiel 38 should be understood within the context of Jewish apocalyptic literature. The War Scroll states the following: "(8)

Capable men for themselves to go out for battle according to the summons of the war, year by year. But during the years of remission they shall not prepare men to go out for battle, for it is a Sabbath

(9)

Of rest for Israel. During the thirty-five years of service, the war shall be waged. For six years, the whole congregation shall wage it together,

(10)

and a war of divisions shall be waged during the remaining 29 years. In the first year they shall fight against Mesopotamia, in the second against Lud's sons, and in the third

(11)

They shall fight against the rest of Aram's sons: Uz, Hul, Togar, and Mesha, who are beyond the Euphrates. In the fourth and fifth, they shall fight against Arpachshad's sons,

(12)

In the sixth and seventh they shall fight against the sons of Assyria and Persia and the easterners up to the Great Desert. In the eighth year, they shall fight against their sons

(13)

of Elam, in the ninth year they shall fight against the sons of Ishmael and Keturah, and during the following ten years the war shall be divided against all the sons of Ham

(14)

According to [their] c[lans and] their [terri]tories. During the remaining decade, the war shall be divided against all [sons of Japhe] th according to their territories."

Thus, many of the same nations identified in Ezekiel 38-39 are also mentioned in the War Scroll. Including the Kings of the North, presumably led by Russia:

"a[nd tile king of; the Kittim [shall enter] Egypt. In his time, he shall go forth with great wrath to fight against the kings of the north, and in his anger he shall set out to destroy and eliminate the strength of

I[srael. Then there shall be a time of salvation for the People of God, and a time of dominion for all the men of His forces, and eternal annihilation for all the forces of Belial."

Absence of the United States in Ezekiel 38

One intriguing aspect of the Ezekiel 38 prophecy is the absence of any mention of the United States. This has led to various theories among Christians as to why the United States is not included in this apocalyptic event. We will cover two of the most popular theories.

One theory suggests that the United States may no longer exist as a significant world power at the time of the Ezekiel 38 War. This theory is based on the assumption that geopolitical shifts and global events could diminish the influence and power of certain nations, including the United States. It is not debatable that we are witnessing this now to some degree. However, the same can be said for many nations across the West and Middle East. Furthermore, the connotations of how this diminishing is happening and why is a point of discussion throughout this work.

Another theory proposes that the absence of the United States in Ezekiel 38 could be due to a strategic retreat or isolationist policy. This theory suggests that the United States may choose not to involve itself in the conflict, either because of political considerations or a desire to prioritize its own national interests. Because of the strong relationship between Israel and the United States since Israel's rebirth as a state, this theory is unlikely. Notably, America's support for Israel spans both the Republican and Democratic Parties, at least to some extent.

While the absence of the United States in the Ezekiel 38 War should not be seen as an indication of its absence from future biblical events or the fulfillment of other prophecies, it is a chilling reality. Ezekiel clarifies that there will not be a single nation to arrive and help Israel. In the midst of the Hamas-Israeli war, we now witness the entire world turning against this tiny nation founded by God.

Conclusion

By comparing the modern nations involved to their biblical names, exploring the connection between the Final Battle of Ezekiel 38 and the Dead Sea Scrolls' War Scroll, and discussing popular Christian theories regarding the absence of the United States, we gain a deeper understanding of this profound prophetic event. Although interpretations may vary, the significance of the Ezekiel 38 War is uncontested. It also serves as a reminder of God's sovereignty and the ultimate fulfillment of His purpose in the world.

I firmly believe that the reason for the absence of the United States is more closely related to geopolitical shifts and global events theory. Still, geopolitical shifts and global events only tell part of the story. With evidence of a strategic multi-part plan engineered by socialist superpowers that I will put forward in this book, I will show what I believe happens to our beloved nation between now and the final battle and why it's not a party to it.

THREE

Chapter 3: The State of the Nation

I ntroduction

The United States of America, a nation founded on Christian principles, has witnessed a gradual departure from its Bible-based roots over time. However, the departure has been much more marked in recent years. This shift has raised concerns among many believers who feel that the nation's diminishing global influence is directly linked to its increasing departure from Christianity and the biblical beliefs upon which it was founded. Furthermore, some worry that certain accepted events and practices in America today are reminiscent of the ancient worship of Ishtar, Baal, and Molech. This chapter explores the diminishing influence of the United States on a global level, the nation's departure from Christianity, and the potential consequences it may face in the event of an attack on Israel.

The Diminishing Influence of the United States

The United States has long been regarded as a global superpower, wielding significant influence in various spheres, including politics, economics, and culture. But in recent years, its influence has waned. While multiple factors contribute to this decline, one significant factor is the nation's departure from its Christian foundation.

The Founding Fathers of the United States were deeply influenced by biblical principles, and the country's early laws and values were rooted firmly in Christian beliefs. Over time, there has been a gradual erosion of these principles, leading to a move away from Christianity as the dominant worldview. This departure has had far-reaching consequences, not only within the nation but also on the global stage.

Departure from Christianity

The departure from Christianity in the United States can be observed through various indicators. These include a declining church attendance, a rise in secularism, and a drastic shift in moral values. While religious freedom remains a constitutional right, there has been a growing trend of marginalizing Christian beliefs and practices in public life. This has resulted in the weakening of the moral fabric that once held the nation together.

As the influence of Christianity diminishes, alternative belief systems and ideologies have gained prominence. This has led to a cultural change that often strongly contradicts the biblical values upon which the nation was founded. As a result, the United States is grappling with issues such as the deterioration of traditional family values, the devaluation of human life, and the redefinition of marriage and gender roles.

When was the shift?

It is rightly understood from various historical records that the United States of America was founded by early settlers on Christian principles. The early settlers of the 13 colonies that eventually led to the formation of the United States came in search of religious freedom. Hence, they established their colonies based on the ideology of freedom of religion, which they considered an offshoot of Christianity. That is, Christianity was practiced under the thumb of the Church of England. Accordingly, the U.S. Constitution and the Bill of Rights, which form the core legal documents on which the U.S. stands, were all developed on the basis of Christian principles. Hence, the concept of signing freedom of worship and expression into law in the U.S. was cultivated, encouraged, developed, and established with Christianity serving as the principal religion to be practiced by its teeming population.

The slow and gradual path of moving away from Christian beliefs began during the enlightenment period of the early 18th and late 19th centuries. At that time, people were allotted more freedom to follow their own paths. Accordingly, over time, different world views crept into society. The growing population in American society and the increasing democratization of the government led to the development of these views. In addition, scientific and technological innovation greatly commercialized the society. This helped change the focus of the population from Bible-based tenets to science-based notions.

Attorney General Edwin Meese, in his report in 1986, stated that the law should rest on a universally recognized consensus of right and wrong. He believed that the Judaic Christian tradition offered just that as it is had been advantageous to society for such a long period of time. He further stated that the founding fathers did not, by any means, intend that the government should take a neutral stance on religious matters "strict neutrality suffers from at least two major drawbacks. The first of these—one of particular interests to the Department—is that the theory ultimately must ignore the history of the religion clauses. The Founding Fathers may not have agreed among themselves as to the meaning of the religion clauses, but we can be relatively confident that they did not envision strict neutrality. Even Jefferson, who was responsible for building the "wall of separation" higher than Roger Williams intended, sponsored legislation as a Virginia legislator that furthered religion, and in his post-presidential days advocated accommodation of religion... in 1787 Congress enacted the Northwest Ordinance in which it declared that religion and morality were necessary to good government." United States. Dept. of Justice. Office of Legal Policy).

The number of Americans who claimed to be Christian was quite high in 2007 but has been on a steady decline since then. We can confidently pinpoint the shift away from Christianity around this time. Palo Alto staff (2015) highlighted some ways that led to society moving away from religion over the past generation via their research. First, they discovered that the number of Americans who felt that one must believe in religion to have good values had drastically reduced from 2010 to 2015. A comparative analysis of the research figures showed that only 30 % of the respondents thought that religion was needed to maintain good values in 2015 as opposed to 49% just five years prior.

Looking back, the early United States Supreme Court often indicated that the religion and government of the United States of America were inseparable. An example of this comes from a ruling by the court during the late 1800s " *Church of the Holy Trinity v. United States*, 143 U.S. 457 (1892).

This meant that the various functions of the government were based on the principles of religion. However, based on the figures of some Nordic nations on the prevalence of Christianity around the same time, some researchers projected that moving away from Christianity was the future of the Western view, of which, of course, America forms a major part. Unfortunately, they were right. By the early 1960s, a Supreme Court case on Bible reading in public schools summed up this drastic change " *Abington School District v. Schempp*, 374 U.S. 203 (1963).

The government has increasingly started questioning the practices of the Abrahamic religions and passing laws that negate the core tenets of them. An example is the issue of same-sex marriage, which was legalized in America and is now another major thorn in the flesh of many Christian wedding officiants. In 2022, President Joe Biden signed legislation that protected gay marriage in the event that the current conservative majority Supreme Court overturned the 2012 case that permitted it in all states. At the ceremony, Vice President Harris spoke about officiating a gay marriage between two women in San Francisco. These examples are a far cry from the early Christian values of the nation.

Ancient Worship and Modern Practices in America

Some Christians argue that certain accepted events and practices in America, including those protected by law, bear resemblance to the ancient worship of Ishtar, Baal, and Molech. While Rabbi Jonathan Cahn is well known for his works on this topic, and I must impart credit where it is due, I first learned of these particular deities while reading the *Dictionary of Deities and Demons in the Bible* (Van Der Toorn et al., 1999) some years ago. In the text, Ishtar also appears alongside the Sumerian deity Inanna. The deity is heavily associated with cities and the glorification of destruction and war. She is the goddess of sexuality, sexual desire, prostitution, feminization, masculinity in females, and the morning star (Van Der Toorn et al., 1999).

If these ancient deities are indeed at work, and the traits ascribed to Ishtar alone would certainly seem to point to the likelihood that they are, perhaps this is part of the underlying reason for America being turned over to its enemies. This is, after all, what happened to early Israel when it failed to turn away from its pagan practices. The other two deities, Baal and Molech, whom Israel also worshiped during the time it had moved away from God, are collectively heavily associated with wealth/prosperity and child sacrifice, respectively. Their worship along with Ishtar throughout the Levant historically involved a multitude of immoral and idolatrous practices.

While it is admittedly healthy to approach such claims with some skepticism, it is worth quickly examining whether there are any parallels between the traditional forms of worship of these deities and aspects of modern American culture. The prevalence of materialism and the pursuit of wealth in American society can certainly be seen as a reflection of the worship of Baal, the ancient god of wealth and prosperity. America is, after all, known globally for its greed and overindulgence. In addition, the acceptance of practices that devalue human life, such as abortion and euthanasia, may be seen as a modern manifestation of the worship of Molech, the same god affiliated with broiling children alive in brass bulls in scripture.

Finally, Ishtar is commonly seen as the embodiment of lust, and her followers were often known for changing their gender through castration and ritual prostitution, which was often homosexual in nature. The explosion of pornography, acceptance of the gender spectrum, and openly proud lust-filled homosexual parades in the last decades, could all easily be accepted as proof of Ishtar's worship and influence in modern America. The same could be said of the mass influx of people into cities, feminism, and the widespread wars of the last century.

Potential Consequences

The departure from Christianity and the embrace of alternative belief systems have raised concerns among believers in Christ about the nation's future. An ever-growing debt, record rates of homelessness, and a drug epidemic fueled by Chinese fentanyl make America nearly unrecognizable compared to just thirty years ago. In particular, these factors and others concern Christians about the nation's ability to withstand threats, both militarily and economically. Much the same as when God allowed Israel to be taken into captivity, the same could happen to the United States as its enemies patiently await to seize the opportune moment, causing internal mayhem in the meantime. In addition, many Americans question the country's ability to respond to not just domestic attacks but also to attacks against Israel or even Taiwan.

Since the rebirth of Israel, the United States has been a staunch ally, often providing military and economic support, as it has been during its War with Hamas. However, the diminishing influence of the United States, coupled with its internal divisions and shifting values, may impact its ability to effectively respond to an attack by a Russian-backed Iran. The same would apply to an attack by China on Taiwan. I believe that if such an attack did occur, the most that the U.S. could afford or would be willing to offer Taiwan would be funding and possibly a limited amount of weapons. These issues naturally raise questions about the nation's commitment to its allies and its ability to defend its own interests, both at home and abroad.

Conclusion

The diminishing influence of the United States on a global level is inarguably a complex issue with multiple contributing factors. One of these factors, perhaps chief among them, is the nation's move away from Biblical values. I put forward this viewpoint, not just because of my own faith, but because it was when Christianity became a minority religion and the U.S. began observing and legally protecting pagan practices that the door for the enemy was made wider. Since then, a downward spiral in nearly all aspects of the country has been constant and with increasing velocity.

Only through unity and renewed commitment to our Christian heritage can the United States regain its moral compass, begin to rebuild, and positively impact the world once more. The diminishing influence of the United States should serve as a wake-up call for us Christians to actively engage in the cultural, political, and spiritual spheres more often. It is imperative that we uphold biblical principles and values and at least try to promote them where we can before they are all but lost entirely and along with them our nation. Although I fear that the current state of America may indicate it is too far advanced in the arrogation process to totally reverse it, God does perform miracles at his choosing. If nothing else, our efforts can at a minimum contribute to the restoration of the nation's Christian foundation and we can try to help shape a brighter future for both the U.S. and all who benefit from it, including our children and Israel.

FOUR

Chapter 4: Global Antisemitism

M ass Antisemitism in Today's World

Antisemitism is, unfortunately, not a new phenomenon in the world. It has been present throughout history and has been the driver of some of the worst acts of violence and genocide conceivable. Likewise, in the modern era, antisemitism has been at the root of some of the most odious hatred without due cause and this has reached an alarming new height during the recent conflict between Israel and Hamas: a conflict that is likely to spill over into Lebanon and possibly beyond sooner rather than later.

While the Jewish people, like all people, are not perfect, Gaza and Hamas unquestionably bear a deep-seated hatred of otherworldly origin. Thus, they bear responsibility for a long cycle of violence committed against the Jewish nation.

Thousands upon thousands of rockets fired indiscriminately and unprovoked into Israel over the course of years, and entirely without aim, is viable evidence of this.

They cry that the "Zionists" are committing genocide, yet Israel has a large population of Muslim Palestinians and Arabs living comfortable, productive lives within its borders. This tells a different tale. Meanwhile, it is Palestinians who have long openly stated that they don't want a single Jew living in the land. In fact, they often put forth that they don't want the Jews living at all. This, combined with the multitudes of unaimed rockets meets the definition of genocide. They are actively trying to remove a people, the Jewish people, from the earth, and they're using deadly violence to accomplish their task. Sadly, this and so much more is clearly lost on many of today's youth and Palestinian or Hamas supporters. They are the same who can often be seen holding signs and protesting Zionism or Israel, chanting "from the River to the Sea" at universities across the West, but they simply don't know enough about the conflict or its history to be protesting at all.

Israel, in large credit to its patience and tolerance, has offered the Palestinians their own separate state seven times in total over the years, but each time to no avail. Multiple peace agreements between the two countries have been repeatedly breached by Palestinians who chose violence instead of peace and diplomacy. Then Hamas carried out its brutal terror attack on October 7th, 2023, that led to Israel's invasion of Gaza. Somehow, while Israel is trying to defeat the terrorist organization parked on its doorstep that is bent on death, rape, and destruction, most of the world will hardly even label Hamas as anything other than "freedom fighters". A bright red sign of the times without question.

Antisemitism in Self-styled Christians in Europe and the U.S.

True Christians are acutely aware that Jesus, our Lord and Savior, was Jewish. All the first Christians were very much Jewish. They observed Shabbat and the laws of the Old Testament. Real Christians are aware that the Bible strictly instructs us to Bless Israel and that if we do so, we too will be blessed. We also know that God's decrees and covenants are without expiration.

However, as contradictory as it may be, many who call have called themselves "Christians" are antisemitic. Two prime examples of these false believers are the Nazis and members of the Ku Klux Klan, who would often cite the crucifixion as the cause for their hatred of Jews even though it was carried out by Pagan Romans. Thus, a contradiction of the highest order: unreasonable, unbiblical, and illogical.

Although the unfounded hatred of Jews dates back to well before the Spanish Inquisition, the term "antisemitism" was not coined until the late 19th century, sometime after the beginning of Christian denigration and persecution of the Jewish people. This antisemitism has taken many forms, from genocide to discrimination in business, and from beating to burning; it is a scourge on the earth that God will rectify in time.

A large number of people worldwide hold profound prejudices against the Jewish people and it's hard to measure as many prefer not to indulge their personal sins. Since the start of the Hamas–Israeli War, the number has likely at least tripled. Thomas Kolsky (2014) writes about what he terms as a perfect Christian prejudice in his book Jews against Zionism: The American Council for Judaism, 1942–1948. He and others define Christian prejudice as a combination of traditional antisemitism and the rejection of the modern nation of Israel on religious grounds.

Kolsky (2014) posits that this prejudice has grown and developed over time using the analogy of a virus. The virus of antisemitism had taken hold without making victims of those exposed to it. Since its inception, Israel as a nation has been a lightning rod for criticism, and this criticism has grown more intense over the years. Most notably since October 7th. Up until that point, there had never been such a large multi-national group of antisemites proudly spewing their hatred. Even during World War 2, the Nazis were confined to Germany. Using Kolsky's analogy, the new Jewish hatred is a new disease, or a new variant spreading faster each day and it's much more severe than the older variants before it.

Much of the world still claims to believe that Israel has a right to security within its own borders, and the right exists to fight against those entities and individuals who would violate its security. It is overwhelming, however, from a Christian point of view that the fight between Israel and Hamas has resulted in such an intense anti-Semitic backlash from essentially every nation on earth. But the invasion of Gaza has illuminated many things that the West was not aware of, such as the Nazi indoctrination of Gazan school children that was occurring at least since Hamas took power and possibly even before.

It now appears that the same indoctrination may be common among many Muslim nations. Among the multitude of articles condemning Israel for defending itself against Hamas at Al

Jazeera.com, one writer wrote "Al Jazeera urges the international community, media freedom organizations and the International Criminal Court to take immediate action to hold the Israeli government and military accountable for these acts of carnage and crimes against humanity." ("Al Jazeera Condemns Israeli Forces Killing of Cameraman Samer Abudaqa"). This statement is a clear indication of the nature of the conflict for large numbers of Muslims who have openly turned against Israel and those who support it. For a short period since the signing of the Abraham Accords, there were considerable progress being made. An example was the Israeli-Saudi Arabian deal that was nearing completion. But since Israel's invasion, that progress has reversed or simply turned to ashes.

Israel's struggle with the Palestinians is also a struggle with ideology, and this is a large part of the hatred and vitriol that has been produced by this conflict. Of course, it is not only within the confines of Palestinians that this problem exists, but also across Europe. European antisemitism is a significant problem, and Jews have been the target of hate crimes in Europe for centuries "Antisemitism is a "deeply ingrained racism in European society" that poses an existential threat to the continent's Jewish community" ("Antisemitism is Deeply Ingrained in European Society, Says EU Official").

Norway is often hailed as the most antisemitic nation in Europe and possibly even the West. Meanwhile, Holland just recently opened a Holocaust Museum, although about three-quarters of Dutch Jews were killed under Hitler. These examples of anti-Semitic sentiment are representative of the climate in Europe, where Jews feel threatened for their safety. Many are afraid to attend synagogue or to be seen dressed in their traditional clothing.

The current conflict between Israel and Hamas has significantly raised tensions in Europe, primarily because there are large numbers of Muslim immigrants in the countries that are most virulently anti-Semitic, including the aforementioned. The recent conflict between Israel and the Palestinians has motivated a host of activists and artists to turn their ire toward Israel in essentially every facet. Boycotting Israeli goods, funds, academics, and conferences has become de rigour as a statement against Israel for quite literally defending itself. But in their demented minds they don't see things this way.

"For approximately 1,900 years, the relationship between Jews and Christians had been marked by anger, hate, and suspicion, particularly in Europe. The primary cause of this lamentable phenomenon was the commonly held Christian belief that Jews were responsible for the death of Christianity's founder, Jesus Christ. This charge of deicide was both extremely inflammatory and an unfair accusation" (Marendy, 2005). Marendy's statement is determinative as to just how long the Jewish people have been prosecuted by European "believers" and by the church. Unfortunately, this antisemitism continues to endure among self-professed Christians and is undergoing a reinvigoration. It's an entirely misplaced and ungodly hatred that disregards not just empathy but God's own everlasting covenant with the Jewish people.

Support for Israel Withdrawn by the United Nations

Before the 1970s, the United Nations was relatively supportive of Israel's existence and rights as a sovereign nation. Within the past 40 years, however, support for Israel within the General Assembly in particular has been slowly eroded. Naturally, this has worsened immeasurably since 2023.

Since last October, the U.S. alone has blocked three resolutions against Israel according to U.N. data. All of the European countries that the nations of the world would typically look to for leadership and a sense of fairness voted in favor of the resolutions. Following its supposed negative treatment of the Palestinians, Israel has been increasingly seen as a nation that violates human rights and the Geneva Conventions, and it has been deemed a threat to regional, and even global peace by the U.N.

It is, perhaps, this twisted perception that led those tens of thousands of people to mount social media campaigns, predominantly via Twitter, under the hashtag "HitlerWasRight" (#HitlerWasRight) in the early days of the conflict. The expansion of this satanic campaign beyond the borders of the U.S. may be seen as likely because it is traditionally the one country that offers consistent support of the nation of Israel, but it is still disheartening. Natan Sharansky's seminal work Defending Identity (2008) posits the belief that Western Europe and Western Europe's institutions, such as the liberal church in the U.S. and Western Europe, have lost their sense of identity and have, therefore, become even more firmly convinced of their own tolerance and worth (Sharansky, 2008).

While it is not appropriate to say that the tolerance of the Western European nations has been snapped up entirely, it is still quite amazing that the issues that the nation of Israel faces and the demonstrations against that country by those "tolerant" Western Europeans have been so prevalent. In the context of this chapter, it is notable that the secular nations of Western Europe do not often support the nation of Israel out of a principled sense of right and wrong but rather because many of those nations still feel guilty about the Holocaust (Sharansky, 2008). This is likely the sole reason many Western nations had not fought against Israel and Zionism with even more fervor until the conflict began.

But that has recently changed. Among the anti-Zionism protests across Europe, the BDS campaign is gaining momentum, and companies doing any sort of business with Israel are feeling the pinch of boycotts and divestments. "Divestment" is often used in the same breath as the BDS (Boycott, Divestment, and Sanctions) campaign against Israel as a means of forcing the nation to "change its behavior". By changing its behavior, the campaigners mean to allow the Palestinians to bomb, torture and kill Jewish Israelis unanswered and not build on the land promised to them by God.

Further examples of modern E.U. sentiment toward Israel is that in 2002, synagogues in Toulouse, France, had to be protected by authorities from arsonists after being firebombed. A similar incident occurred in Belgium in 2014 when a synagogue was set afire in four places ("European Jewish groups call for better security"). There has been a string of similar and much more recent events across the E.U. since of the fall of 2023, but the former examples show the attitude toward Jews that was already in place.

China and Russia: Support for Hamas

The two socialist superpowers that have dominated the world state of affairs in the past century, Russia and China, perhaps without surprise, have come down on the side of the Palestinians against Israel throughout the history of the Middle East. This choice is hardly surprising, since both Russia and China are socialist nations and have large Muslim populations in the countries or areas under their control. Socialism very much historically aligns with antisemitism as we will see in the next chapter. Additionally, China has moved into the Middle East and negotiated a deal between Iran and Saudi Arabia while Russia obtains munitions and drones from Iran. Since the historic attack by Hamas, the two have made their positions abundantly clear concerning Israel.

What is surprising, however, is the little resistance that China has received for its cruel treatment of the Uighur Muslims within its borders, where the group is frequently placed in internment camps or often murdered in mass. Remarkably, the world's "China is off limits" rule is even well-established in the United States. Last year, an NBA basketball player stated that he quickly found himself without a contract for raising the Uighur issue. Yet, China can somehow freely denounce Israel for defending itself against terrorists as though it has a moral high ground. The power that Russia and China are able to project, even against Western efforts, are directly contributing to the global influx of antisemitism. They are actively pushing the Muslim narrative especially where that narrative might also be conceived as anti-American.

Conclusion: Make a Stand

Christianity is a religion founded by a group of Jews who believed that one person, Jesus of Nazareth, another Jew, was the Son of God made flesh and the prophesied Messiah of the Hebrew Bible. His historical name, after all, was Hebrew: Yeshua Bin Yosef. While it is not the primary driver of religious hatred (that disgrace belongs to Islam by and large), Christianity, as the professed faith of many who oppressed Jews during the medieval period of antisemitism, is left with a duty to protect and care for the group of people who have endured more than their share of hatred and violence.

Now would be a great time for any who calls themselves Christian and who shares even a modicum of antisemitic sentiment to repent, discard it, pray about it, and stand up for Israel. It is, after all, the same Israel that God declared would exist again and would bless the world through that very existence. As prophetic events continue to unfold and the Jewish state finds itself continuously more secluded, it needs our support, the true Christians, now more than ever.

FIVE

Chapter 5: Communism & Socialism

I ntroduction

Communism, a sociopolitical ideology founded by Karl Marx, has been a subject of controversy and debate since its inception. This chapter sheds light on the dark side of communism, highlighting its inherent evils, corruption, and brutality. By exploring its history, core tenets, and the impact it has had on societies, we will delve into the reasons why communism is incompatible with Christian values and provide some signs that there is a current communist movement behind the scenes working to take control of America.

History of Communism and its Devastating Consequences

Communism traces its roots back to the 19th century, when Karl Marx and Friedrich Engels authored the Communist Manifesto. This ideology gained momentum during the Russian Revolution in 1917, which led to the establishment of the Soviet Union. Soon after, the ideology reached China and led to the establishment of the People's Republic of China, often referred to as the PRC.

It is estimated that tens of millions of people lost their lives under the Soviet and Chinese communist regimes "61,911,000 people were murdered by the Soviet Union, 38,702,000 by the Chinese communists" (Rummel, 2011). The mass deaths were primarily due to forced collectivization, political purges, and subsequent famines. The latter is believed by some Christians to be punishment from God due to the regimes' atrocities. Regardless, these tragic events highlight the destructive nature of communism and the total disregard for human life that it engenders. Additional examples of such disregard for human life include the communist-style human-wave battle strategy that led millions of soldiers to slaughter in World War II and China's one-child policy, which only recently ended.

Core Tenets of Communism and its Connection to the Illuminati

Communism advocates the abolition of private property, the control of the state's means of production, and the establishment of a classless society. It also advocates for the abolition of religion "*communism* is not only irreligious but antireligious" (Smith, 2019). The reason is because it simply cannot tolerate a higher authority than the state. Eerily though perhaps not at all surprisingly, these principles align with the core tenets of the historical secret society known as the Illuminati.

The society was founded in 1776 by Adam Weishaupt who "believed that society should no longer be dictated by religious virtues" (Vickery, 2017). Like the founder of communism, the founder of the Illuminati also hailed from Germany, a historical hotbed for antisemitism. Marx was well known for his deep disdain for the Jewish people (Bloom, 1942). Both ideologies behind communism and the Illuminati seek to centralize power, suppress individual freedoms, and promote a globalist agenda.

Relationship between Communism and Socialism

Communism and socialism are often used interchangeably although they are technically somewhat distinct ideologies. I do, however, use the terms interchangeably throughout this work. While communism advocates for the complete abolition of private property and the establishment of a classless society, socialism seeks to achieve economic equality through government intervention and wealth redistribution. In reality, modern communism is socialism.

Although it claims to be a communist nation, China, for instance, has rallied about its unique form of government that is based on socialism. First coined by Deng Xiaoping in 1982, "the concept of socialism with Chinese characteristics aims to redefine the relations between planning and socialism, and market economy and capitalism. It has preserved institutions of socialism and public ownership while importing sophisticated management experience and

advanced market mechanisms from developed countries."
(CGTN). In truth, there are no truly communist government
systems today (Encyclopedia Britannica).

However, both ideologies share the common goal of
challenging traditional religious institutions and placing the
state above religion. Communism and socialism also claim to
prioritize the collective over the individual faith. In reality,
stripping away any faith held by subjects besides that placed
in the government makes a population far easier to control.

Signs of a Socialist Takeover in the United States

Identifying signs of a communist or socialist takeover in the
United States requires a nuanced understanding of political
dynamics. As alluded to in the title to and earlier in this
work, there is compelling evidence, which I will present later,
that suggests that America's two greatest enemies have been
slowly implementing a plan to arrogate the nation. Their plan
has been a mostly subtle but consistent one, and we can now
see the final pieces moving into place. Each day, the
conclusion draws nearer. These are some indicators that
their plan not only exists but is nearing fruition:

a) Government Control

The expansion of government control over various sectors of
the economy, such as healthcare, education, and industry, can
be seen as a step toward socialism. The primary driver of
government control is via rules hailing from federal agencies.
Between 1995 and 2016, nearly 90,000 federal rules were
codified. In 2016, there were almost 4,000 rules issued, but
only 217 laws were enacted by the president and Congress
(Crews, 2017).

It is worth noting that these figures only reflect federal administrative rules and not those issued by state agencies, which can sometimes be matched in number. For example, the California Code of Regulations contains the regulations of roughly 200 state agencies. "But these things matter no matter who's president, because increasingly, since the federal government is so pervasive, it can regulate private activity without waiting for Congress to pass a law, and without even going through the normal notice-and-comment rulemaking process to which agencies "must" adhere. That threatens conservative and liberal values alike." (Crews, 2016).

This excessive state intervention has stifled individual liberties and grossly undermined the free market. How can a capitalist nation succeed when a free market is crushed by regulations? Simply put, it cannot. If the regulations continue to strangle the free market as they have been, any part of it that remains will be doomed to fail. When it does, it will affect all Americans save for perhaps the elite without bias.

b) Erosion of Individual Rights

The erosion of individual rights, such as freedom of speech, freedom to bear arms, freedom of religion, and assembly, is another indication of a shift toward socialist authoritarianism. These constitutional rights are fundamental to the American democratic society. They should be safeguarded at all costs.

c) Redistribution of Wealth

Policies that advocate excessive wealth redistribution without considering individual merit and hard work can be seen as aligning with socialist principles. While addressing income inequality is important, it should be done in a manner that encourages individual initiative and rewards productivity. Yet, somehow, as the national debt balloons to absurdly extreme levels, the top one percent only becomes increasingly wealthier while the federal and state welfare systems continue to give freely to the willfully unemployed. Simultaneously, the middle class continues to shrink more and more each day as it nears extinction.

d) Disregard for Traditional Values

The undermining of traditional values, such as the importance of family, faith, and personal responsibility, is another serious indicator of the nation's cultural shift toward socialist ideologies that prioritize the collective over individual liberties.

Conclusion

From a Christian perspective, communism and socialism stand in stark contrast to the values of love, compassion, and respect for individual dignity that are central to the Christian faith. Today's flavor of communism is in reality a form of socialism, but the elements of violence, oppression, suppression of religious freedom, and authoritarianism all still remain intact. Unfortunately, there are very real indicators that the United States is not only under attack by socialist powers but that their plans, decades at work, are nearly complete. However, by understanding the inherent evils, corruption, and brutality of both ideologies, we as Americans and Christians can still fight back by actively engaging in promoting Biblical values such as justice, freedom, the value of truth, and the dignity of our fellow men and women.

SIX

Chapter 6: Russia: Goals & Control

I **ntroduction**

This chapter provides insight into how the Soviet Union and later Russia have long planned and worked to influence the United States government and its population. We will also examine how modern Russia is, in fact, a socialist nation. As a quick reminder, we have covered earlier, modern communism is technically socialism but generally under dictatorial rule, as seen with Xi's China. Therefore, we can understand that Russia is by default a modern communist nation under Vladimir Putin.

Finally, we will look at indicators showing how Russia already has control over the U.S. in some very important respects. These are, of course, only the overt indicators, as it is both difficult and inherently dangerous to know precisely how deeply Russian control truly runs within our government. This is frequently referred to in modern society as the deep state. However, I personally prefer the term dark state because with conspiratorial connotations aside, although Russian control runs deep, it is easily visible on the surface if we know where to shine the light. There is also an underlying darkness to it as I think the case is with any form of communism. Later in this work, we will examine actual compelling evidence of both Russian and Chinese control within our federal and some state governments.

To avoid confusion among younger readers, I refer to Soviet Russia as Russia and vise versa. This seems appropriate because Putin, and much of his government, were Soviet communist officials before the collapse of the U.S.S.R. Likewise, most Russian population was born and lived many years during the Soviet era. This golden era of communism is a powerful and recent memory to most Russians, many of whom, especially those in the current administration look back on with favor.

Russia is Still a Socialist State

During the Cold War, the U.S. and Russia did not have a similar perspective on the war. The U.S. seemed to have a somewhat lax view of communism for much of the period, although perhaps this was intentional during certain presidential terms. In an attempt to achieve its objectives in post-war Europe, in Yugoslavia, the U.S. was able to support the Tito regime, which was fighting under the communist revolutionary Josip Broz. Let this also serve as an example of a somewhat lax view of communism. While the U.S. was trying to help Europe rebuild after the war, Russia had plans to take over.

Russia was the undisputed cradle of European communism and has remained so until now. Each of the communist bloc nations was loyal to and organized under Russia. Thus, most Russian citizens today take great pride in being associated with it. Socialism, they often claim, means that weaker members are helped at the expense of the strong in a society.

This high sense of national ideology where the citizens believe in socialism could be one of the contributing factors to the rise of the Communist Party and its popularity in the nation today. Russian politics are not as simplified as they are in many western nations. Political parties, especially those without a specific ideology behind them, such as the United Russia Party, can constitute members of every other party. This is because they either support the individual running for office based on his or her goals or plans, or because some parties, such as United Russia, are basically made to include everyone. Thus, United Russia is a Party comprised to do exactly what it sounds like: unite Russia into one Party regardless of individual ideology.

Therefore, many of the Russian Communist Party or CPRF members, in fact over half of them, voted for Putin in 2003 and moved to his United Russia Party. Putin and his ideology appealed to over 60% of the communists in the nation "The Party of power–United Russia–managed to gather the largest portion of the popular vote and secured a constitutional majority in the State Duma. The Communists lost up to 60 percent of their electorate."... "The electoral support of United Russia" "consists of many types of voters from all major political parties... The opposition parties continued to lose support in the last legislative elections. The decrease in the Communist voting base can be attributed to the massive migration of CPRF [Russian Communist Party] voters to the United Russia." (Kunov et al., 7-8).

As you can see, Putin's Party, United Russia, is indeed itself a Party with modern communist elements and members. It is a Socialist or modern Communist Party in every respect but in name. What's more, even the formally titled Communist Party is rapidly growing within Russia due to Putin's inclination for war, although it must officially remain second due to voter fraud committed at Putin's direction "Yet, according to official preliminary voting results, the Communist Party won the precinct with nearly 29 percent of the vote, followed by 20.3 percent for the ruling United Russia Party. The Gulag museum polling station results indicate a surge in strength for the Communist Party of the Russian Federation (KPRF), which is set to gain 15 seats in the new State Duma, the lower parliament house, according to preliminary official results from elections marred by evidence of fraud."... "In short, United Russia is set to take 72 % of the Duma seats after polling just under 50 % of the Party-list vote, while the second-place Communists will have 12.7 % of the seats with 19 % of the vote." (Coalson).

Obviously, the United Russia Party is simply a rebranding of the Communist Party that ruled the Soviet Union. President Gorbachev believed the same "Former Soviet President Mikhail Gorbachev calls it "a bad copy" of the Communist Party that ruled the Soviet Union for seven decades" (Weir). Similarly, the Russian economy is very much a modern communist or socialist economy. "The Russian state remains large and pervasive. All liberalization indices show that the Russian economy is far from liberal, and corruption thrives on excessive regulations. As President Yeltsin (1999) put it in his Annual Address to the Federal Assembly on March 30,

1999: "We have got stuck half-way in our transition from the planned and command economy to a normal market economy. We have created a hybrid of the two systems." (Aslund, 1999).

Russian Goals to Arrogate the United States

Since the establishment of the Soviet Union in 1922, it has ceaselessly focused on penetrating the United States government and influencing the public. Every successive leader of the Soviet Union, from Vladimir Lenin to Boris Yeltsin, has striven to gain control over the United States government in some form. The inception of socialist and communist movements in the United States posed an opportunity for the Soviet Union to attain its goal.

In recent decades, Russia has been increasingly acting to infiltrate the United States government to the extent of interfering with the 2016 presidential election as well as the 2018 and 2020 elections (Ignatius, 2021). It has also used a host of other measures to make the United States seem inferior to the rest of the world. There are few avenues that Russia has not at least tried to explore in its quest for dominance over America.

Due to the sensitivity of the topic, I would like to quickly clarify that I am not stating that Russian interference is the reason that former President Donald Trump won the 2016 election. There was an inquiry, and he was found not to be associated with any form of Russian interference. Trump won the 2016 election because he was a vastly popular candidate at the time, and he remains so today. However, I am stating that Russia did put forth a concentrated effort to steer the 2016 presidential election, specifically toward the Republican Party, and it has continued to do so.

Likewise, China is guilty of the same. In fact, China recently interfered in the 2022 Midterms to increase support for candidates from both parties that it considered Pro-China (De Luce, 2022). Although historically, China has favored politicians belonging to the Democratic Party, and Russia most often appears to favor Republican Party members. Influence from Russia and China targeted at the highest levels of the American government is not at all biased. Likewise, the U.S. government and the wealthy elite that are compromised by the socialist powers are not limited to party lines. However, those powers repeatedly prey upon the two-party system as a tactic to widen the divide among Americans.

Another exemplary example of Russia's goal is the Kremlin's plan to control the entirety of the Internet: "the United Nations has embraced Russia's proposal to write a new treaty governing cybercrime, to replace the 2001 Budapest convention that Moscow rejected because it was too intrusive. Second, Russia is lobbying for its candidate to head the U.N.'s International Telecommunications Union (ITU) and use it to supplant the current private group, known as ICANN, which coordinates Internet addresses.", "These international regulatory battles sound obscure, but they will help determine who writes the rules for Internet communications for the rest of the 21st century. The fundamental question is whether the governance process will benefit authoritarian states that want to control information or advocates of openness and freedom." (Ignatius, 2021). If Russia's plan succeeds, all information that is shared on the internet across the world would be subject to dictatorial style censoring and suppression. A worrisome fact is that negotiations for the Kremlin's proposal are still underway even after the invasion of Ukraine. Unsurprisingly, its main ally in the fight is China.

Consequent to Russia's indiscreet activities regarding elections, the American public has become aware of the Kremlin's rising influence. Thus, the majority has a negative perception of Russia because of its involvement in the country's foreign affairs. Unfortunately, this majority is shrinking due to the latest efforts it has put forward regarding misinformation and weaponizing the Republican Party divide over Ukraine. But more on that later.

In reflection, Russia has in fact intended to take over the United States government since the early Cold War, and in lockstep with China, it is now well on its way. One of the reasons that seem to nurture this intention is communist sentiments. The need to infiltrate, conquer, and dismantle capitalist democracies is an unrelenting goal of communism and socialism, and there was no larger trophy to be won than the U.S. This is because America was the greatest example of a capitalist democracy in the world. It is still a great example of democracy, but we will cover that more in depth in another chapter.

Russian Interest in the U.S.

For over half a century, Russia was considered by most the arch enemy of America. During the Cold War, the two superpowers fought some indirect wars in which the U.S. turned to Western European countries to offer a counterforce to the Soviet Union. In short, the U.S. adopted a policy of containment (Friedman, and Friedman, 23). This, turned out to be highly inadequate. Although America tries to take credit for the Soviet Union's collapse, the real reason that it failed had much more to do with itself than any external power.

According to Friedman and Friedman (21), after the fall of Soviet communism, America began openly showing some level of goodwill where the two countries were working together for a common goal. In contrast, Russia has used a cunning face where it has been working hard to further its hidden agenda of gaining control over the United States. This is because Russia has never perceived America as anything other than its enemy: a threat that required neutralization. The evidence lies in the fact that Russia has for many years developed and stockpiled weapons of mass destruction whose primary target was always the U.S. Pipes (80) stated that while the West developed these weapons for deterrence, Moscow developed them for an offensive. Of course, Russia had help from Washington D.C. to aid it in its objective.

The Kremlin still consistently tries to develop an array of future weapons that will give it an upper hand over the U.S. Considering these efforts, America has frequently gone overboard providing Russia with aid that it has took and used to develop its arsenal. In reality, America has contributed many times to its own undoing. For example, when the U.S. bailed Russia out from its Afghanistan War, Russia emerged stronger in terms of its weaponry. Considering that Russia had so much Soviet era military equipment that was still operable, at least up until the invasion of Ukraine, it allowed it to pour more money into developing advanced weapons that NATO had no answer to. A prime example of this is its hypersonic missile, which it claims is unstoppable by any missile defense system currently available.

Most American officials were unaware that just since 1991, billions of dollars in U.S. aid to Russia (Wedel) would go on to advance the nation's weapons technology. However, the number of officials in Washington who were willfully furthering the agenda of the socialist superpower were all too aware of where the money was going and can take credit for their part in this twisted achievement. Even those who were unaware had no response to Putin's revealing himself as a corrupt dictator "A fan of Mario Puzo's *Godfather* novels will still see the Putin government more accurately. Looking at the regime's insistence on strict hierarchy, unquestioning clan loyalty, and a stern code of secrecy, plus its taste for extortion and supreme urge to keep the revenue flowing at all costs, this observer will see the regime for what it clearly is: a mafia. Until recently, the regime wore a thin coat of democratic paint. At the start, Putin believed that this was necessary to maintain membership in the G8 and other democratic clubs and to keep his oligarchy's money safe in Western banks. But after years of cracking down on democratic institutions in Russia with little or no reaction from Western leaders, Putin realized that he could dispense with the charade." (Kasporov, 2009).

Besides the billions of dollars in U.S. aid, you may be tempted to ask where Russia has found additional money to finance these projects being as weapons research and manufacturing can get expensive. "In the middle of the river, local mafiosi cut deals that will arm Taliban insurgents in southern Afghanistan, as well as al-Qaeda and other militant groups in the wider region. In return for Russian-made weapons, they trade Afghan heroin that will eventually be sold on the streets of European cities." ("Turning Afghan Heroin into Kalashnikovs"). The Afghan heroin is then smuggled into the U.S. and sold by the Russian or Sicilian mafia. This is strikingly similar to what we are seeing now from China and its fentanyl operations in conjunction with Mexican drug cartels. "Mexico and China are the primary source countries for fentanyl and fentanyl-related substances trafficked directly into the United States," ("Fentanyl Flow to the United States"). Not only does this strategy weaken the U.S. population via an addiction epidemic, and a resulting health epidemic, it causes the deaths of thousands of Americans. There is also a lot of profit to be made which is then used to help finance Russian and Chinese state projects such as weapons development.

According to various reports from several government agencies and Russians themselves, it is most often the FSB, the Russian Federal Security Services, who are only pretending to be the Russian mafia. This notion coincides with the following excerpt from the Federation of American Scientists' Intelligence Resource Program "In New York, the LCN (La Cosa Nostra) and Russian organized crime figures have formed working relationships", "On September 8, 1993, several Russian crime figures were arrested in St. Augustine, Florida for conspiracy and intent to import 800 kilos of cocaine. The Russian group was dealing with Costa Rican drug traffickers and had plans to smuggle a large quantity of cocaine from Colombia" (Russian Organized Criminal Activities in California).

Due to Russia's covert influence in Washington, D.C., the U.S. has previously allowed Russia to acquire certain essential satellites that would undoubtedly expose the U.S., where in the event of a real war, Russia would take advantage of this decision. Currently, Russia is working to build anti-satellite weapons. Thus, if a ground war did ignite between the East and the West, these weapons would be used to destroy NATO satellites severely crippling Western forces. Meanwhile, the Russian satellites gifted by the U.S. would provide a monumental advantage all but guaranteeing a Putin and Xi victory. The resulting destruction to the West would be incalculable.

Furthermore, Russia has been able to gain control over the U.S. and Europe through its energy sector. Even now, two years into the Russia– Ukraine War, America continues to pay billions of dollars for Uranium to Russia's Nuclear Agency (Bearak, 2023). The E.U. has also dropped its Russian gas imports by only one third. Although both Europe and America have raced to stop importing Russian oil, Russia still has a stranglehold on enriched Uranium as the Rosatom Corp., an entity controlled by the Kremlin, supplies about half of the fuel for the world's nuclear power stations (Tirone, 2023).

Russia's Partnership and Cooperation with China

The Chinese and Russian relationship can be traced back to the early Cold War days when the two nations stood together against the western alliance spearheaded by the U.S. During those days, most of the countries of the world were still underdeveloped and had an issue of self-identity. The two countries saw the challenge as an example of the West determining if and when they failed along with the consequences it would entail. As a result, on the issue of national identity, instead of siding with Western countries, China sided with demographically large and underdeveloped Russia as it saw that the latter was better placed to suit China's needs.

This relationship can be seen when Russia repeatedly tried sabotaging agendas put forward by America as a world power.

For instance, when America intervened in the Korean War, China saw it as a dangerous act that might one day be a stumbling block to its national growth and development. As a way of trying to salvage the situation, China started to work closely with the Soviet Union to protect its borders. In so doing, this marked the beginning of the Sino-Soviet Treaty of 1950.

The resulting alliance is one that has existed until today with a limited number of disagreements. Of course, the Chinese–Russian relationship has grown markedly since the early days of the 1950s. Russia's invasion of Ukraine, China's aggression in the South China Sea, its disapproval of Israel defending its nation against Hamas, and its constant threats toward Taiwan all share an obvious commonality: the unfailing support of each socialist dictator for the other. This was proudly put on display for the world to see when Putin and Xi confirmed their no-limit partnership, which included military cooperation and closer economic ties.

With the changes in the world since the early Cold War, the dynamics in the relationships of the major players have dramatically changed. For example, if someone were to visit Russia currently, even during the present time of war, they could be excused of thinking that they were in America or any other Western European nation. Even during wartime, the cost of food in Russia is very affordable even by Western standards.

On the other hand, China has made some almost unbelievable economic strides since the 1990s. Its economy now easily rivals that of the U.S. and even exceeds it in some ways as we will see in the next chapter. Both China and Russia are powerful and are growing. The threat they pose to the West is greater than ever. The nations are involved in issues of Central Eurasian fuel and security, seeking to counterbalance U.S. power, and forming cooperative relationships with energy-rich states in the Middle East.

They almost seem to be mirror images of each other in all but the size of their GDPs, population, and demographics. Taking into consideration the fact that both countries are taking on large projects, each have or are planning for a war, and both are exerting an increased African and Middle Eastern influence, China and Russia are closer than they have ever been. Their interests seem totally aligned, and Putin and Xi like to make the world aware of it.

Conclusion

With the rise of Russia after the Second World War, the United States first employed containment policies that were grossly ineffective. The Soviet Union expanded to a vast area and included many European, Balkan, and Central Asian nations. The USSR collapsed due to its own policies combined with some resistance from the West, and soon after, the U.S. began providing aid to Russia. The nation, still communist by modern standards, went on to use billions of dollars in American aid to further its primary goal of taking over America. It still uses U.S. money for enriched Uranium for the same purpose.

China and Russia, with a historic relationship between them, are both firmly anti-American and anti-West. They both now seek to increase their global influence and expand the power of their communist regimes. Both have allied to some degree with America's most dangerous enemies, such as Iran, and both are at odds with America's allies, such as Israel. The two are closer than they have ever been, and a severely weakened U.S. remains the largest obstacle on their path to world domination.

SEVEN

Chapter 7: China: Goals & Control

I ntroduction

China's remarkable economic growth and expanding military capabilities in recent years have positioned it as a global superpower. China boasted the world's largest population until recently. The nation's army, or People's Liberation Army (PLA) has nearly 3 million personnel as of 2024. It is by far the largest on earth. Likewise, its Navy (PLAN) is the largest navy with nearly 400 vessels, and it is still growing ("What is Most Significant in the Pentagon's China Military Report?"). Due to an increasing defense budget, PLA forces continue to receive upgraded equipment and advanced technology, as Xi says he is preparing the nation for war (Pomfret and Pottinger).

China's rise has been a topic of interest and concern for many countries in the West, particularly the United States. In this chapter, we will delve into China's meteoric economic rise, its growing military strength, and the implications of both. We will also look at some examples where China has demonstrated its intentions of exerting its influence over the United States and its goals in undermining it. Furthermore, we will analyze China's current efforts to assert its dominance on the world stage and what its belt and road initiative might mean for the future of America.

China's Economics Rise and Military Superiority

China's economic transformation over the past few decades has been nothing short of extraordinary. Through a combination of market-oriented reforms and strategic planning, China has become the world's second-largest economy in terms of GDP. However, when adjusted for price difference, known as purchasing power parity (PPP), China has been the largest economy in the world since 2014. Its GDP growth rate consistently outpaced that of the United States, leading to a rapid increase in its economic power.

A PPP-adjusted GDP analysis performed by PWC showed its projections for the world by the year 2050. In its projection, three of the four top world economies will be Asian. China will be ranked number one with 20% of the world's GDP, India second, the United States third, and Indonesia fourth. Further, our European allies will be replaced in the top 10 by Turkey, a key Russian and Chinese ally, another communist nation, and the Central American nation that plays a crucial role in China's fentanyl operations: "UK could be down to 10th place by 2050, France out of the top 10 and Italy out of the top 20 as they are overtaken by faster growing emerging economies like Mexico, Turkey and Vietnam, respectively" ("World in 2050").

According to PWC, the E7 countries, that is, China, India, Brazil, Indonesia, Mexico, Russia, and Turkey, were equal in adjusted GDP as the G7 in 2016. The G7 includes the United States, United Kingdom, Canada, Italy, France, Germany, and Japan. In just fifteen years, the GDP of the E7 is projected to amount to double that of the G7. ("World in 2050").

The expected drop in global PPP adjusted GDP in the United States is from 16% in 2016, to 12% by 2050. A shocking 25% reduction. What's more, is that a sharper decline of 40% is projected for the E.U., which, as per the report, will fall from 15% as of 2016 down to 9% by 2050.

Russia is expected to remain steady in the sixth position, although the effects of the Ukraine war had not been factored into the analysis. However, given its 1.1% projected GDP increase for 2023 ("IMF Datamapper") during an active war, China's predicted rise and the close relationship between the two nations will likely keep Russia's GDP steady and the projection accurate. Meanwhile, Brazil, another founding BRICS member alongside India, is projected to move up two spaces to the fifth largest PPP adjusted GDP ("World in 2050"). These numbers all currently align with the International Monetary Fund's latest data, which has all G7 nations at an expected 1% or less in GDP growth rate. Meanwhile, the data has China's expected growth rate at over 4% and India's over 6% ("IMF Datamapper"). Thus, so far, PWC's projection seems quite accurate.

China's military capabilities have also grown exponentially. China has boasted the world's largest standing army for years and has made significant advancements in areas such as cyberwarfare and space technology. Meanwhile, Xi Jinping continues to make substantial investments in modernizing the nation's armed forces and securing food in anticipation of war with the West "in March, (2023), Xi wove the theme of war readiness through four separate speeches, in one instance telling his generals to "dare to fight." His government also announced a 7.2 % increase in China's defense budget, which has doubled over the last decade, as well as plans to make the country less dependent on foreign grain imports" ("Xi Jinping Says He Is Preparing China for War").

Historical Instances of China's Ambitions toward Arrogation

To fully understand China's desire to exert influence over the United States, we must examine historical events and statements made by Chinese leaders. As we have already seen in the previous chapter, China and the Soviet Union have been partners since the 1950s, except for some minor temporary disagreements. During the Cold War, China, under the leadership of Mao Zedong, expressed its revolutionary ideology and desire to challenge the Western capitalist order. The communist state adopted a strategy of aligning with the Soviet Union to counter the United States' global influence, a strategy that Xi has reanimated with some ferocity.

Mao frequently referred to the United States as an imperialist nation, and imperialism was a concept that he, just like the Bolsheviks he admired, strongly opposed. Mao's famous quote, "The east wind prevails over the west wind," encapsulated China's aspiration to surpass and subvert American influence. Although admittedly, during this period, China's primary focus was on consolidating its power domestically and asserting its influence in Asia as is standard order in any nation with aspirations of growth. Yet, given the projection report from PWC and the Beijing-aligned forces within our nation's government, Mao seems to have been proven correct.

Still, Mao's feelings toward the United States continue to linger in China. In the communist cradle of Asia, Mao is considered to be a revolutionary hero, and Chinese youth are indoctrinated with his ideology starting at a very young age. Xi, who is often compared to Mao, is now continuing the red hero's revolution as Xi's iron grip tightens further around the nation. "Since he came to power in 2012, Party enforcers have punished roughly five million people for offenses as serious as abuse of power and as innocuous as creating excessive red tape" (Wong).

China's Current Efforts to Assert Internal and External Dominance

In recent years, China's ambitions have become more apparent as it seeks to challenge the United States' global leadership. China's Belt and Road Initiative (BRI), a massive infrastructure project spanning numerous countries, is seen by many as a means to expand its influence and create a China-centric global order. With nearly 150 nations now being a part of the initiative, China has concretely established that order ("Countries of the Belt and Road Initiative").

Concerning China's cyberwarfare capabilities, it has waged a host of cyber-attacks against the U.S. and NATO allies in the past year. Among the targets was a U.S. defense industrial base: "September 2023: A new Microsoft report indicates an increase of Chinese cyber operations in the South China Sea, as well as increased attacks against the U.S. defense industrial base and U.S. critical infrastructure. The increase comes amid rising tensions between China and the United States" (Center for Strategic and International Studies).

In addition, China has been assertive in territorial disputes in the South China Sea, leading to tensions with neighboring countries and the United States. The Chinese government has also drastically increased control over its domestic population since Xi took power. It is often referred to as a surveillance state, and for good reason. Its obsessive use of technology for surveillance purposes attests to that. Likewise, its 2019 move to digital currency assists in China's control over the population. These shifts have raised concerns about the erosion of democratic values and human rights within the nation.

Conclusion

China's rise as a global power has undoubtedly impacted the United States and the West at least to some degree. While there have been historical instances where China expressed its desire to challenge the influence of the United States, it is essential to consider the broader context and China's evolving strategic priorities. It first wanted to build its domestic, regional, and intercontinental capabilities before specifically targeting the U.S., as it is now.

China's economic growth and military capabilities have positioned it as an extremely formidable competitor to the United States. Its current efforts to assert dominance through initiatives such as the BRI and assertive actions in disputed territories cannot be ignored by the uncompromised officials in D.C. if there is to be any hope at slowing America's arrogation. As our nation tries to navigate the changing global landscape, and due to the national debt and other core issues, it is important that those officials try to find a median of stability and strength with China.

EIGHT

Chapter 8: Evidence: Sowing Seeds

I ntroduction

Up until this point, we have covered the Ezekiel 38 War and the nations mentioned within it. We have seen that Russia will lead the group of nations against Israel and that the United States will not be able to answer the call to defend its ally. We have also examined the essential components needed to understand the threats Russia and China pose, the underlying dangers behind those threats, and discussed their shared goals of taking over our nation as well as the origin of those goals.

I have covered several very real signs that our country is far along in its transition into a socialist regime while the American people have been distracted by politics, questions of gender identity, sports, and climate change. I have stated on multiple occasions that the United States' conversion from a beacon of democracy to a socialist state began decades ago via treasonous forces buried deep within the highest ranks of our federal government. Next, I will go over the types of evidence to better understand what I have included in this and the next chapters. We will also see what evidence is admissible at court to comprehend the value of that evidence, and finally review the evidence I have collected and put forward to prove that the arrogation process has been underway for nearly a century.

Circumstantial Evidence

In federal courts and the courts in every U.S. state, there are two types of evidence, these are direct and indirect. Direct evidence links a person directly to a crime or civil wrong. Examples of this type include eyewitness accounts and testimony by someone who claims to have personal knowledge of the incident ("Direct Evidence").

Indirect evidence, also referred to as circumstantial evidence, indirectly links a defendant to a crime or civil wrong. Both however serve as legitimate proof that a crime has been committed. A criminal conviction or civil judgment in court can be obtained using only circumstantial evidence. It is actually the most often used type. "One commonly used form of evidence in criminal and other cases is circumstantial evidence. In fact, most of the evidence used in criminal cases is circumstantial.. Circumstantial evidence is indirect evidence that does not, on its face, prove a fact in issue but gives rise to a logical inference that the fact exists. Circumstantial evidence requires drawing additional reasonable inferences in order to support the claim. For instance, circumstantial evidence of intentional discrimination can include suspicious timing, ambiguous statements, different treatment, personal animus, and other evidence can allow a jury to reasonably infer intentional discrimination." ("Circumstantial Evidence").

Thus, examples of circumstantial evidence can include timing that is deemed to be suspicious, a statement that may have more than one meaning, a person's intent or will, and indirect testimony. Further, it can include documents. Neither direct nor circumstantial evidence are given more weight than the other by courts "Both kinds of evidence are a part of most trials, with circumstantial evidence probably being used more often than direct. Either kind of evidence can be offered in oral testimony of witnesses or physical exhibits, including fingerprints, test results, and documents. Neither kind of evidence is more valuable than the other." ("How Courts Work").

Of course, changing a nation from a free democracy to a communist nation is not in itself illegal. It would be considered as simply the evolution of a nation's type of government. A government official secretly working for a foreign state however would be. Yet, most people were blind to the reality staring back at them during the period this chapter and the next cover, much the same as the majority of people are today. As I mentioned before, distractions are inherently useful to mask reality. Still, there were some people with their eyes open and they realized what was taking place. Among them, included the U.S. Supreme Court, U.S. Senators, and Congressmen.

Of course, the circumstantial evidence presented in this work will not be used at court even if there were a court who had the jurisdiction and desire to hear such a case. But it is important to note that the evidence covered in this, and the following chapters would be admissible. Further, it would be deemed by a court to be just as valuable as direct evidence.

Interview with a Soviet Spy

In 1984, Yuri Bezmenov, a Soviet KGB officer who had defected to Canada completed an interview on live television. His most terrifying claim was that Russia was implementing a long-term strategy of psychological warfare and "demoralization" in order to defeat the United States. Although it will take decades to succeed, as we have already seen, the long game is certainly paying off.

Bezmenov emphasized that, contrary to what contemporary popular culture may suggest, the KGB does not primarily engage in espionage in its operations. Eighty-five percent of the effort involved "a slow process which we call either ideological subversion, active measures, or psychological warfare." ("39 Years Ago, a KGB Defector Chillingly Predicted Modern America."). Next, we will examine the proof that Bezmenov was not only right, but that Russia and China have had help all along from those within the highest tiers of our government.

The Beginning: Sowing the Seeds of Marxism

Evidence that Former President Franklin Roosevelt had a Socialist Agenda and Contributed to the Arrogation of the United States

Pt I: Recognizing the Enemy

Former President Franklin Delano Roosevelt, or FDR, is often remembered as the president who pulled America from the Great Depression. His New Deal did stimulate the economy, and he certainly should receive credit for his role in aiding the nation in its recovery. However, he was accused by many to be a communist or socialist and this chapter will work to prove that he in fact did harbor socialist ideologies which are largely reflected in his policies. When doing preliminary research about FDR being a socialist, you will mainly find that those who made the same argument during Roosevelt's lifetime were far-right oriented. Yet, as the history of World War II has taught us, fascists were firmly the arch enemy of communists and so this is not at all surprising. Still, this was not by any means the rule.

One of these accusers who admittedly did fall beneath the umbrella of the far-right was Gerald L. K. Smith. Smith believed that Roosevelt and his advisers were all communists. Although sadly, he was openly antisemitic and held racist opinions, like many others during the time, Smith is often quickly dismissed due to his ideological preferences. However, he did not officially join the Nazi-like group known as the Silver Shirts as preliminary research may lead you to believe. In fact, at least on the face, some organizations Smith was associated with appear to be quite the opposite to those typically associated with the far-right.

One such organization was the Union Party and included both Republican and Democrat Party members. The Vice-Presidential nominee and Presidential nominee of the Union Party was District Attorney Thomas O'Brien and U.S. Representative William Lemke, respectively. The fiscal position of the party was best described as left-wing and the social position as that of the center-right. Thus, the party was a long way away from being considered far-right.

"Opposing President Franklin D. Roosevelt, the party chose North Dakota Congressman William Lemke as its standard-bearer. Smith said he was proud to speak not only for Lemke but also for the Constitution, the American flag, and the Bible. The Smith-Townsend-Coughlin collaboration faltered because of personal rivalries, and Lemke's candidacy failed. Smith continued his agitation, founding several vehicles to fight communism." ("Smith, Gerald Lyman Kenneth").

Smith also joined the Share Our Wealth Society and was appointed as its National Organizer. The society was a group that helped promote the idea that the wealth in America should be shared and was opposed to FDR's New Deal reforms. United States Senator Huey Long planned to base his 1936 presidential campaign on the idea, and he was set to challenge FDR in the race. At least, that is until he was assassinated in late 1935. It is not known with certainty whether FDR was behind his murder, but considering his policies and associates, I think it is entirely possible.

Not all who accused Roosevelt of being a socialist or a dictator belonging to the far-right. Some, such as William Randolph Hearst, were considerably well-rounded ideologically. Hearst owned the New York Journal, and he was a U.S. Representative. He had also belonged to the Democratic Party early in his career but was firmly republican during Roosevelt's term. Hearst had some very strong words regarding FDR "On September 21, 1936, newspaperman William Randolph Hearst attacked FDR in his newspaper, *The New York American*. He accused the President of being a Socialist, Communist, and Bolshevik and wrote that FDR was carrying out a Marxist agenda." ("September, 1936").

Pt. 2: New Deal Reforms - Making a Socialist State

There were also many in government who were opposed to FDR's reforms. Most believing that it was a far overreach of both presidential and congressional power. Among those opposed were the conservative justices of the United States Supreme Court, which FDR managed to manipulate through fear in his favor.

The dire situation of the Great Depression created the perfect atmosphere to usher in new government control. Americans were so worn down at the time due to extreme levels of unemployment and food shortages that they were willing to accept extreme government intrusion in exchange for stability and sustenance. Many people who lived in Eastern Europe during the Soviet communism era state that this was often the reason that citizens capitulated. They were so worn down from hardship caused by the aftermath of World War II that they could no longer keep fighting to prevent communism from taking hold. It was very similar circumstances during the Great Depression.

Thomas Jefferson and James Madison, two of the most famous of the nation's founding fathers, each had a limited perspective on the government's spending power. They believed that it was not enough for federal spending to be tied to the general welfare but instead, it had to fall within the means of executing a specific enumerated power granted by the Constitution. Thus, if the power was not granted, the executive branch had no authority to act under the Constitution.

As the Supreme Court wrestled with Franklin Roosevelt's New Deal, Jefferson's, and Madison's constrained viewpoint once more appealed to the conservative majority of the court. Roosevelt's spending plans threatened the idea of limited federal spending power and were at least as ambitious as his regulatory reforms. To try to maintain some degree of restraint on that power, the Supreme Court struck down a major New Deal program expenditure initiative in 1936. However, in a fear-based response to Roosevelt's court-packing scheme, which would allow him to appoint 6 more justices, the court changed its position the next year. The episode was so intense that the court didn't strike down another statute that would limit federal spending power for over 75 years. In 2012, the court finally partially invalidated the Affordable Care Act's expansion of Medicaid.

A large part of the New Deal reforms brought on by FDR was the creation of a host of administrative agencies, many by executive order. But because there was also a democrat majority U.S. legislature, FDR could push through any legislation he pleased. Thus, some agencies were also created by congressional act but all at FDR's direction. Estimates place the total number of administrative agencies created during FDR's time in office at around 70. 20 of those were created just during his first year as president.

This gave rise to the administrative state that endures today and continuously adds more regulations in every industry. Many Americans would rightfully later become worried about the power the agencies had to create and enforce their rules without any input from the public. Congress enacted the Administrative Procedure Act of 1946 in response. However, it was merely a band aid on a bullet wound. The act allowed and still allows for federal agencies to issue and enforce rules without hardly any participation from the public and the agency heads are not elected by the people.

In the same way as the federal spending power, the Supreme Court also sought to limit the commerce power as it believed many of FDR's reforms were unconstitutional. In a case called *Schechter v. United States*, all justices, even the liberal justices who would often sympathize with FDR, ruled against the codes required under the New Industrial Recovery Act (NIRA). The case concerned the four Jewish Schechter brothers who followed the laws of Kashrut and adhered to the humane treatment of animals. The brothers owned two kosher butcher shops and allowed customers to visually inspect chicken before purchasing. NIRA regulations enabled the government to control which chicken customers could buy which went against the brothers' business model. The Schechter brothers didn't obey the regulations and were sentenced to 3 months of jail time as well as steep fines.

From the Bill of Rights Institute regarding the *Schechter* case "Chief Justice Charles Evans Hughes wrote the opinion for the Court and asserted that despite the crisis of the Great Depression, "Extraordinary conditions do not create or enlarge constitutional power" ("National Recovery Administration and the Schechter Brothers"). "The law had allowed the government to exercise unlimited authority and sanctioned a "completely centralized government... Moreover, the Court thought the legislative branch had unconstitutionally delegated its authority to regulate interstate commerce to the executive branch and so had violated the principle of separation of powers" *Id.*

When the case was argued before the Supreme Court in early May of 1935, defense lawyer Joseph Heller explained the new law to the astonished justices. Heller argued that the law was "destructive of our dual system of government and subversive of our political, social, and economic institutions under the Constitution." *Id.* Heller was very aware of what NIRA meant for the nation and the importance of the government's role in the economy, particularly in a capitalist country.

The National Recovery Administration (NRA) was created by FDR via executive order to carry out NIRA. Its official logo was a blue eagle clutching a gear in one foot and three lightning bolts in the other. The lightning bolts were eerily reminiscent of the logo of the American Socialist Worker's Party founded in 1938. The logo I am referring to is available at the Granger Historical Picture Archive's website. Perhaps the underlying meaning behind the NRA symbol was the institution of a socialist machine. Afterall, that is in essence what Roosevelt and the agency did.

General Johnson was appointed to head the agency and claimed that it was optional for businesses to follow the NRA codes while simultaneously telling customers to only buy from stores that proudly displayed the NRA logo. However, as NRA was created to carry out NIRA, it was thus found to be unlawful by the Supreme Court in the *Schechter* case in 1935. Sadly, legislation enacted by the democrat led congress and senate would soon after incorporate many of its provisions ("National Recovery Administration"). The NRA directly manipulated the economy by creating false food scarcities in order to increase prices and in turn increase profits. Government price fixing is a control tactic very often utilized in command economies, which are otherwise known as communist economies.

Former Congressman Hearst had similar opinions regarding the NRA "Not all were pleased, however. Journalist William Randolph Hearst said the program was an example of state socialism and quipped that NRA stood for "No Recovery Allowed." ("National Recovery Administration and the Schechter Brothers"). Another critical journalist, Walter Lippmann, asserted "The excessive centralization and the dictatorial spirit are producing a revulsion of feeling against bureaucratic control of American economic life." Some business owners began to agree with those sentiments." *Id.*

The following is extracted from the U.S. History Organization:

"The New Deal was clearly the most ambitious legislative program ever attempted by Congress and an American President... Progressive politicians saw their wildest dreams come alive... This amount of regulation and involvement requires a vast upgrading of the government bureaucracy...

An armada of government bureaus and regulatory agencies was erected to service the programs of the New Deal. Collectively, observers called them the "ALPHABET AGENCIES... The NRA, like the AAA for farmers, attempted to create artificial scarcity with commodities. The hope was that higher prices would yield higher profits and higher wages leading to an economic recovery...

In 1933, Roosevelt asked Congress to create "a corporation clothed with the power of government but possessed of the flexibility and initiative of a private enterprise." The Tennessee Valley Authority was born, and economic recovery came to eastern Tennessee...

To avoid charges of SOCIALISM, the NRA allowed each industry to draw up a code setting production quotas, limiting hours of operation, or restricting construction of new factories. Once the President approved each code, pressure was put on each business to comply. A PROPAGANDA campaign reminiscent of World War I ensued...

There seemed to be no end to the alphabet soup. The SECURITIES AND EXCHANGE COMMISSION (SEC) was created to serve as a watchdog on the stock market. The FEDERAL HOUSING AUTHORITY (FHA) provided low interest loans for new home construction. The HOME OWNERS LOAN CORPORATION (HOLC) allowed homeowners to refinance mortgages to prevent foreclosure or to make home improvements. The UNITED STATES HOUSING AUTHORITY (USHA) initiated the idea of government-owned low-income housing projects." ("FDR's Alphabet Soup").

You may be thinking that there are many similarities between China under Xi Jinping, the Soviets, and FDR's administration. Yes, there certainly are. Among them include a disguised corporation that was secretly owned by the government, an agency that was artificially driving up food prices to effect the economy, a sprawling bureaucracy, work related quotas which required the president's approval, government jobs, cheap government loans for home builders, propaganda campaigns, an Office of Censorship, and the construction of government owned low income housing reminiscent of soviet bloc style apartments. Indeed, there are many similarities.

When FDR allowed the federal government to control or command the economy, the U.S. economy was effectively changed from a capitalist economy to a socialist blended economy. It remains one today "The United States has a mixed economy. It works according to an economic system that features characteristics of both capitalism and socialism. A mixed economic system protects some private property and allows a level of economic freedom in the use of capital, but also allows for governments to intervene in economic activities in order to achieve social aims and for the public good." (Ross).

Recall that the Great Depression took twelve years in total to correct. Within the three-year span between the beginning of the depression and FDR's arrival in office, the majority of Americans would have been so worn down from hardship and the accompanying stresses that they blindly accepted FDR's communist policies that were taking place. Most were even grateful for them. The resulting mound of national debt left behind from the New Deal was probably not even a factor in their minds. Again, I will admit that FDR's reforms did in fact aid a lot of Americans during the Great Depression and prevented a multitude from starvation. But at an inconceivable expense to capitalism and American freedom.

Pt. 3: U.S. as a Social Democracy and its Prophetic Implications

A fascinating, yet somewhat concerning fact, is that as we seen previously, since Roosevelt's reforms the only occasion that the Supreme Court has challenged the federal spending power was in 2012. Again, this was in response to Former President Obama's Affordable Care Act (ACA) Expansion. Obama, much like FDR, was in office as a result of the Great Recession of 2008 and likewise, the ACA was a large part of his reform. Further, during this time there was also a democratic majority in the house and senate, acting at Obama's pleasure, just like during the New Deal. This may simply be a strange coincidence, as history does so often repeat itself, but it is fascinating to consider, nonetheless.

When the Great Depression finally did end, a second world war began soon after. While many do fear a physical war with Russia and China is on the horizon now, I do not believe this to be the case. Or, at least, not in the way the prior world wars occurred. I think that as far along into the process of arrogation our nation now is, a physical war is simply not necessary for our enemies to secure their victory. They essentially already have.

I believe that the arrogation of America will be completed by means of an increase of Asian economies, the decrease of Western economies, and the further destruction of our social, cultural, religious, and moral systems. The combination of these, carried out by Russia and China, has already greatly reduced America's soft power throughout the world. Because of this, I believe that the next global war will either directly give rise to or will be the Ezekiel 38 War itself.

Capitalism, socialism, and communism are all defined by and center around a nation's economy. The key characteristics of both socialism and communism rests on the command economy in which the government has control over it in some meaningful fashion. Once this occurs, a nation is no longer capitalist by definition.

Therefore, before FDR came to office, the United States was a capitalist nation. During his presidency, America became a socialist state. Many laws have certainly been put into place over the years since the 1940s but none that have reverted our economy back toward capitalism from a mixed capitalist-socialist economy. We do however, at least for now, still retain the democratic process. Thus, America has been a social democracy since and because of Franklin D Roosevelt.

More still, as arrogation continued onward over time, we have moved closer toward becoming a strictly socialist nation. The next rung on the ladder is a democratic socialist nation. I and many political analysts believe that the U.S. is already there primarily as a result of the Biden administration. Unfortunately, our country will move even closer toward becoming a communist state in preparation of the arrival of the Antichrist. The mass control it will entail will be a requisite for the conditioning of the population.

Pt. 4: More Evidence Pointing Toward FDR's Role in the Arrogation of the U.S. by Russia and China

Former President Roosevelt's role in the transformation of America from capitalism to socialism has been covered in some depth in this chapter. Thus, I will only briefly summarize the remaining evidence proving the seeds were sown toward the arrogation of our nation by a former sitting President of the United States who wielded a hidden communist agenda. Most of the sources the following excerpts are taken from are from government or government tied websites.

A Note on Excerpts: I have included a lot of excerpts in the chapters on evidence for a few reasons. First, is that I wanted to quote the sources directly so that my own personal opinion is not in question. This is important because evidence should rely on the opinions of the external sources and not a summarization that is subject to personal bias. Second, is so that this book will contain a record of the text from the sources I have cited. It is important to preserve the texts so that in the event of any possible future government censorship, the source's text won't be changed to fit a political or social narrative. Most websites are updated periodically. I have personally seen the text contained within them change in order to align with a certain political or government agenda being pushed at the time. Thus, the excerpts provide a lasting record of the evidence that was available when this book was written. Last, briefly describing the evidence then including the quoted text from an external source that you can read for yourself will make for more focused reading. It will also allow for painting a clearer picture of the scenario when taken in whole. Finally, let's begin...

1. FDR's Close Relationship with Armand Hammer- FDR was friends with Dr. Armand Hammer, the son of Julius Hammer who was a founding member of the American Communist Party.

A. Both Julius and Armand were being monitored by MI5 and MI6 as suspected Soviet agents:

"Julius HAMMER / Armand HAMMER: Russian, American. A founder member of the American Communist Party, Julius HAMMER came to notice in the 1920s as being in contact with a person suspected of transmitting funds to the USA for revolutionary purposes and as the founder of several companies believed to be under Soviet control, notably the Allied American Corporation of which his son Armand HAMMER was an official. The London branch of this company appeared to be the financial agent of the Soviet Government for propaganda purposes and the Hammers were associated with a woman known to be an OGPU agent" (The National Archives of the UK. Reference: KV 2/3899).

B. Sworn Statement on the relationship from Former First Lady Roosevelt: "I will not quote from all the records available in the archives, except for a sworn statement by Eleanor Roosevelt: "Not only did I know Dr. Hammer very well in a business way, but I knew him much better socially. He was many times to the White House for dinner ... . Not only do I admire him, but for his great service to our country in the late war, my husband, the President, esteemed him highly." ("Response From Armand Hammer").

C. Armand and two other members of the Hammer family donated in Former President Roosevelt's memory via the American-Canadian Campobello International Park:

"I want to publicly thank Dr. Armand Hammer and Mr. Harry Hammer and Mr. Victor Hammer for their most generous contribution in President Roosevelt's memory, and to his deeply held love for the Canadian people. I think that President Roosevelt would be pleased that this is a new and very special project. It is, as you know, the first jointly owned U.S.-Canadian park. This is ample evidence of a close tie between the United States and Canada." ("Remarks at the Signing of the Roosevelt Campobello International Park Agreement").

"After he became President, FDR returned only three times to the island, but Eleanor and other family members came much more often. In 1952 Eleanor sold the cottage to legendary American businessman Armand Hammer, but ten years later as she neared death, convinced Hammer to deed the property to a joint Canadian American international body that runs it to this day." (Dunlop).

2. Lend-Lease Program- Billions of Dollars in Military Supplies for Socialist Nations including China, Russia, Chile, Brazil, and Peru- The Lend-Lease Program provided the equivalent of nearly $1 trillion today in military supplies to America's "allies". Among them included the Soviet Union and China who each received equipment and supplies worth several billion dollars. The Soviet Union received nearly three times the amount that France received with $11 billion versus $3 billion respectively.

A. The program provided Brazil, a democratic socialist nation that was also under left-winged leadership at the time, $100 million in military aid. Additionally, it provided nearly $20 million in aid to a left-wing led Peru. As of 2021, Peru has been under the leadership of a Marxist-Leninist President.

"By the end of 1942, the [Lend-Lease recipient] list included the Soviet Union, China, Australia, New Zealand, and the governments-in-exile of Poland, the Netherlands, and Norway. Later, the Free French movement under Charles de Gaulle received supplies, as did a host of new Latin American allies including Paraguay, Brazil, and Peru." (Seidl).

B. Chile received $50 million in supplies. FDR had relatives in Chile. His Chilean fourth cousin served as Minister to Washington. In 1941, the country was under the leadership of President Cerda who won office via overwhelming support from the Socialist, Communist, and Radical Parties. President Rios took office the following year and is said to have been even more radical than Cerda. With FDR's cousin serving in such a position of power, he likely would have belonged to the same party as Cerda and held the same socialist views.

"The Secretary of State to the Chilean Ambassador (Michels)

Washington, December 9, 1941.

Excellency: I have the honor to invite Your Excellency's attention to the offer made by the Government of the United States in the interest of hemisphere defense to furnish the Government of Chile [Page 577] with armament valued at $50,000,000. The equipment for this purpose would be provided under the terms of the Lease-Lend Act of March 11, 1941.

The Congress of the United States enacted on October 28, 1941 the Defense Aid Supplemental Appropriation Act.60 Of the funds appropriated under this Act, $150,000,000 have been set aside for the acquisition of military and naval equipment by the other American republics.

The budgetary limitations, however, require that the funds in question shall be obligated not later than February 28, 1942. In consequence of this, it would be appreciated if Your Excellency's Embassy, provided it has not done so already, would be good enough to present to the appropriate authorities of this Government at the earliest possible date the official lists of the desired equipment in order that the necessary action may be taken toward the procurement of this material."

FOREIGN RELATIONS OF THE UNITED STATES DIPLOMATIC PAPERS, 1941, THE AMERICAN REPUBLICS, VOLUME VI. 825.24/270½a.

C. Roosevelt had an excellent relationship with Stalin and that is shown by the following excerpt from the U.S. Embassy in Russia's website:

"Even before the United States entered World War II in December 1941, America sent arms and equipment to the Soviet Union to help it defeat the Nazi invasion. Totaling $11.3 billion, or $180 billion in today's currency, the Lend-Lease Act of the United States supplied needed goods to the Soviet Union from 1941 to 1945 in support of what Stalin described to Roosevelt as the "enormous and difficult fight against the common enemy — bloodthirsty Hitlerism."

· 400,000 jeeps & trucks

· 14,000 airplanes

· 8,000 tractors

· 13,000 tanks

· 1.5 million blankets

· 15 million pairs of army boots

- 107,000 tons of cotton

- 2.7 million tons of petrol products

- 4.5 million tons of food" ("World War II Allies: U.S. Lend-Lease to the Soviet Union, 1941-1945").

3. Immediate Recognition of the Soviet Union After Taking Office-

"*Maxim Litvinov*

On December 6, 1917, the U.S. Government broke off diplomatic relations with Russia, shortly after the Bolshevik Party seized power from the Tsarist regime after the "October Revolution." President Woodrow Wilson decided to withhold recognition at that time because the new Bolshevik government had refused to honor prior debts to the United States incurred by the Tsarist government, ignored pre-existing treaty agreements with other nations, and seized American property in Russia following the October Revolution. The Bolsheviks had also concluded a separate peace with Germany at Brest-Litovsk in March 1918, ending Russian involvement in World War I. Despite extensive commercial links between the United States and the Soviet Union throughout the 1920s, Wilson's successors upheld his policy of not recognizing the Soviet Union.

Roosevelt Pushes for Recognition

Almost immediately upon taking office, however, President Roosevelt moved to establish formal diplomatic relations between the United States and the Soviet Union." ("Recognition of the Soviet Union, 1933").

4. Mao Zedong-

A. Declassified documents revealed that during the latter months of World War II, Chinese Communist leaders Mao Tse-tung (also spelled Zedong) and Chou En-lai offered to visit Washington. They wanted to speak face-to-face with Former President Roosevelt regarding the future of China. However, their message was never delivered to him directly because of a communication error on the part of Ambassador Patrick Hurley.

This is very noteworthy because up until that point the U.S. had supported Mao's opposition during the Chinese Revolution to assist the U.S. against Japan. It is likely that Mao and Chou had taken notice of Roosevelt's communist policies as well as his close relationship with the Soviets and wanted to meet with him. ("MAO ASKED TO SEE ROOSEVELT IN 1945").

B. John Service worked as a diplomat under FDR and was later at the heart of a Pro-Soviet conspiracy in the State Department. He was later purged and prosecuted but received leniency. Federal Bureau of Investigation (FBI) files that were declassified in the 1990s showed that Thomas Corcoran, a New Deal adviser to FDR, requested the FBI to take it easy on Service (Kiffner). Service was hired by U.S. Ambassador to China Clarence Gauss, who was appointed by Roosevelt in 1941.

The excerpts below taken from the Office of Historian shows that Mr. Service did want to provide weapons and training to Mao Zedong and his Communist Party, and the White House was aware of it.

"The Ambassador in China (Gauss) to the Secretary of State

No. 3018

Chungking, September 28, 1944. [Received October 24.]

"In Report no. 16 (enclosure no. 3) Mr. Service suggests that the United States should supply the Chinese Communists with urgently needed military supplies and training in the use of such supplies, to be followed later by actual tactical cooperation. Mr. Service points out that the implementation of such a policy is likely to meet with resistance from the Kuomintang, and suggests that the United States must decide whether the gains which can be reasonably expected to accrue from assisting the Communists will justify the overcoming or disregarding of anticipated Kuomintang opposition. He expresses the view that the limiting of American support and assistance to the Kuomintang alone will not win the United States an effective ally whereas impartial support of the Kuomintang and the Communists will provide an effective force in the latter," ("Foreign Relations of the United States: Diplomatic Papers, 1944, China, Volume VI").

C. Below, Mao stated that he and the Chinese communists wished for Roosevelt to be re-elected.

"Memorandum by the Second Secretary of Embassy in China (Service) of a Conversation With Mao Tse-tung

[Yenan,] August 23, 1944.

"First, is there a chance of an American swing back toward isolationism and a resultant lack of interest in China? Are Americans [going to ?] close their eyes to foreign problems and let China "stew in her own juice"? We Communists feel that this problem will not arise if Roosevelt is re-elected." ("Foreign Relations of the United States: Diplomatic Papers, 1944, China, Volume VI").

Conclusion

Former President Roosevelt's reforms undoubtedly prevented the starvation of countless Americans. However, they also birthed the administrative state and effectively converted the United States from a capitalist nation into a socialist nation, which it remains today. FDR's policies added a third to the national debt in just three years of his presidency. Many of the New Deal reforms and policies were not only inexcusable but clearly served to further the agenda of our country's most dangerous enemies. As we have seen, communism is all about the long game.

After FDR passed away in 1945, the next several presidents in office either left the New Deal reforms in place or even expanded them. That is, until Former President Gerald Ford took office. Former President Reagan too would later greatly help push the nation back toward capitalism as a call to deregulate the economy in the mid-1970s to early 1980s led to the dismantling of much of the socialist regulations that had begun with Roosevelt. Those same regulations only worsened during the early 1970s as we will see next. More still, many of FDR's agencies remain intact today and the U.S. still retains its mixed capitalist– socialist economy that FDR instituted.

NINE

Chapter 9: Evidence II: Nixon

I ntroduction

Due to the Watergate scandal, and being the only U.S. President to resign from office, there has been much speculation regarding former President Richard Nixon. He is often portrayed as a victim by Roger Stone, a lobbyist and former adviser to Nixon. According to Stone, former President Kennedy was a communist who sought to assassinate Nixon and planned to carry out the assassination via the Central Intelligence Agency (CIA). The evidence shown in this chapter will tell a very different story as to who the communist really was.

On the surface, I think most people would initially believe that the victim is usually the man who was actually assassinated. Not just because of the assassination itself, but also because Kennedy didn't get to spend decades after leaving office striving to save his legacy and his reputation. In addition, Kennedy was the president who nearly went to war with the Soviets. That war would have almost certainly involved nuclear weapons. Accordingly, the arguments made by Stone regarding Kennedy's war profiteers making money from a Soviet-American war are simply not feasible.

A weapons business cannot profit when the nation it resides in and sells the weapons to has been decimated by nuclear bombs. The resulting currency would hardly be worth the paper it's printed on, and then, how would the profiteers spend the money? I don't think the CEO of any major weapons manufacturer would necessarily want to spend the next 50 years locked in a concrete bunker nor would he deem such a scenario to be a success.

Then again, Stone almost braggingly stated that Nixon's campaign was funded by "mob money". I have wondered whether that money came from the Russian mafia itself or from the Italian mafia. As we have seen, La Cosa Nostra and the Russian mafia do indeed have a partnership and have for some time. We have also seen that the Russian mafia are most often Russian intelligence agents in costume. I don't believe Stone realized just how much his statements could be used against Nixon when he made them.

While Kennedy was on the brink of catastrophe with the Soviet Union, and I, like most, am happy that it never happened, Nixon capitulated to the communist powers on more than one occasion. Often, his capitulations even angered our European allies. The evidence provided in this chapter proves that Former President Richard Nixon was in fact working alongside both China and Russia to help them realize their communist agendas and accomplish their eventual goal of the arrogation of America.

Evidence that Former President Nixon had a Socialist Agenda and Contributed to the Arrogation of the United States

1. Henry Kissinger-

A. Henry Kissinger has a long and interesting past. He served as both the National Security Adviser and the Secretary of State under Nixon. He was, right up until his death, a friend to Xi Jinping. Kissinger was invited to spend time with Xi twice while in China during the bitter President Trump Xi Trade War.

"Henry Kissinger met in China with President Xi Jinping, and the details of his conversations were passed onto President Donald Trump, White House economic advisor Larry Kudlow tells CNBC.

Kissinger met with Xi twice during a weeklong trip to China, along with "other big shots," Kudlow says. Kudlow says shared Kissinger's dispatch with Trump.

Xi told Kissinger he would rather deal with Trump than Democrats, who "will go on about human rights and other things," according to Kudlow." (Breuninger and James).

B. When Kissinger was serving under Nixon, he ordered to have the intelligence links severed between the National Security Administration (NSA) and British Intelligence. Doing so would have left the U.S. in the dark on Middle East intelligence as it was Britain who single handedly supplied it to the U.S. If the NSA had complied, Kissinger's order would have prevented the U.S. from learning of the Soviet invasion of Afghanistan just 6 years later. I'm willing to bet this was not a coincidence.

"British and U.S. signals intelligence are so tightly bound that the two agencies are more loyal to each other than their own domestic leaders, according to "Behind the Enigma."

"I say in the book—and both GCHQ and NSA allowed me to say it—that at some point or another, every director of GCHQ and NSA colludes with each other in order to do something which their own national authority might try to impede," Ferris told The Daily Beast.

One such clash arose in 1973 when Kissinger, who was President Nixon's national security adviser at the time, ordered the NSA to stop sharing signals intelligence with Britain in order to pressure London to support Nixon's Israel policy.

The NSA refused to comply, challenging Kissinger's authority despite his key role at the White House. Ironically, under the shared intelligence agreement between the agencies, Kissinger's move would have left the U.S. flying blind in the Middle East because collecting signals intelligence in the region was entirely the domain of the British who funneled the intel back to Fort Meade.

One of the most bizarre aspects of this unparalleled intelligence sharing partnership is that it is not enshrined in any treaty; it's a subnational, totally non-binding agreement, which makes the NSA's willingness to stand up to Kissinger even more extraordinary." (Hines).

2. Nixon's Swift Withdrawal from Vietnam- During the time of the Vietnam War, nothing would have made the Chinese and Soviet communists happier than the U.S. pulling out of Vietnam. They wanted the U.S. to stop supporting the democratic South Vietnamese so that the communist North Vietnamese could take over the country. The wanted communist rule without opposition. Pleasing Russia and China, Nixon wasted no time in this regard. He also ended the draft which created a much smaller and less formidable American military.

A. He began to pull U.S. troops out of the war in 1969, the same year that he took office. Nixon completed the withdrawal in 1973, just before his resignation from the presidency. Kennedy had resisted the removal of U.S. troops as he knew it would bolster the communists. Meanwhile, Nixon's withdrawal caused the U.S. and its South Vietnamese allies thousands of casualties due to a weakened force and insufficient supplies.

The following excerpts for subsections A-D are from the Office of the Historian:

"Nixon began to withdraw forces from Vietnam, meeting with South Vietnam's President Nguyen Van Thieu on Midway Island on June 8 to announce the first increment of redeployment. From that point on, the U.S. troop withdrawal never ceased. As U.S. troop strength and capabilities declined, the United States worked toward building South Vietnam's military capacity through a program known as

"Vietnamization." It would remain a constant question over the remaining years of the administration, whether the South Vietnamese could build the combat capability, logistics and planning capacity, and leadership at the national and military levels to face the North Vietnamese on their own." ("Ending the Vietnam War, 1969–1973").

B. Nixon, via National Security Adviser and close friend to Xi Jinping Henry Kissinger, was able to coerce the South into a treaty with the communists which the North swiftly broke. Nixon had threatened to cut off all support to the South Vietnamese if President Van Thieu didn't accept the terms. Thieu was reluctant because he knew the agreement would mean a certain victory for the communists. This is, of course, something that Kissinger and Nixon were both very much aware of.

"Kissinger was unable to find any common ground acceptable to both Vietnamese parties in two renewed rounds of negotiations... Meanwhile he [Nixon] continued to exert intense pressure on Thieu, threatening to cut off U.S. economic, military, and political support of South Vietnam if Thieu refused to accept the agreement." ("Ending the Vietnam War, 1969–1973").

C. After North Vietnam broke the agreement, South Vietnam retaliated, and the war continued until the South's defeat. Nixon assured the democratic South Vietnamese leader that if the communist North broke the treaty, he would respond by sending B-52 bombers. Being as he was furthering the agenda of the North's communist allies, he never did.

"Nixon wrote Thieu that "I repeat my personal assurances to you that the United States will react very strongly and rapidly to any violation of the agreement." Both sides understood this to mean the recommitment of B–52s to combat. In the end, these commitments were not upheld due to a combination of factors—domestic and Congressional reluctance to re-engage in the war, economic constraints, and finally the Watergate scandal, which weakened and distracted Nixon. Having rebuilt their forces and upgraded their logistics system, North Vietnamese forces triggered a major offensive in the Central Highlands in March 1975. On April 30, 1975, NVA tanks rolled through the gate of the Presidential Palace in Saigon, effectively ending the war." ("Ending the Vietnam War, 1969–1973").

D. Nixon and Kissinger was willing to hand over South Vietnam and even cut off aid completely to please the communist superpowers.

"Meanwhile, Nixon and Kissinger sought to reshape the international context of the war through building relationships with North Vietnam's superpower allies in Moscow and Beijing. Nixon wanted to create a dilemma for the Soviet and Chinese—give them "bigger fish to fry," in his phrase—in choosing between their support of North Vietnam, and a closer relationship with the United States. The 1972 summits in Beijing and Moscow reflected this strategy, though the Communist powers continued their material support of Hanoi." ("Ending the Vietnam War, 1969–1973").

E. Sabotage of peace and the use of democratic South Vietnam to win office and hand Vietnam to the communists.

According to Larry Berman, Professor and Director of the University of California Washington Center, Nixon intentionally sabotaged the peace agreement entered between North and South Vietnam. The Paris Peace Treaty seemed to have settled the Vietnamese conflict before Nixon had ever won. But on the eve of the presidential election in 1968, Nixon sabotaged the peace agreement to help oust Former Vice President Humphrey from the race. Professor Berman cites hundreds of declassified documents, wire taps, Kissinger's notes, and even cross-checked the information against North Vietnamese accounts. (Berman, 2001).

"Berman reveals the step-by-step betrayal of South Vietnam that started with a short-circuited negotiations loop, and ended with double-talk, false promises, and outright abandonment. Berman draws on hundreds of declassified documents, including the notes of Kissinger's aides, phone taps of the Nixon campaign in 1968, and McGovern's own transcripts of his negotiations with North Vietnam. He has been able to double- and triple-check North Vietnamese accounts against American notes of meetings, as well as previously released bits of the record." (Berman, 2001).

Nixon undoubtedly had a larger plan at play than simply winning the election. That was to fulfill the wishes of Russia and China. By restarting the conflict, Nixon pretended to be helping South Vietnam in the name of "liberty". Yet, the entire time, his and Kissinger's intent was bent on wearing the South's army down. Then, Nixon would finally abandon President Thieu completely to allow the communist North to take possession of the whole of Vietnam. This also coincides with documents showing that Nixon was aware his bombing campaigns were not at all effective. They were simply a ploy.

An article by the Guardian states that Humphrey and Former President Johnson both knew about the Nixon's 1968 debauchery but had decided not to go public in the interest of the American public (Kettle). In carrying out his detestable scheme, Nixon effectively cost 20,000 U.S. soldiers their lives as well as tens of thousands of Vietnamese and Cambodians theirs. It also prevented what would have been a successful and productive democracy in South Vietnam, likely much the same as South Korea is today. However, Russia and China would have wanted to prevent a second strong capitalist democracy with U.S. ties in Asia at any cost. Nixon obeyed and carried out the orders of the enemy as instructed.

3. Nixon Contributed Largely to the Economic Disaster of the 1970s and Each U.S. Recession Since-

Soon after Nixon's term began, the nation's economy began to suffer. For the first time in U.S. history, stagflation struck. Stagflation is the stagnation of an economy combined with high unemployment and high inflation. This, from an economic perspective, is not something that is supposed to happen as high unemployment usually reduces inflation and vice versa. In combating the new dilemma of stagflation, which was likely engineered as a smoke screen, Nixon put into place policies that have continued to haunt the nation's economy since. They also, not so mysteriously, have boosted the Russian and Chinese economies over time and continue to do so as we will later cover. These policies are collectively referred to as the Nixon Shock.

A. The Nixon Shock.

As we'll see in the excerpt taken from a textbook on economic policy at the University of Houston, while Nixon was engaging in high social spending, foreign competition deriving mainly from Russia was running high. Nixon set a new bar for the nation in controlling the economy by enacting wage and price freezes. These temporary freezes, or controls, for a short time converted the U.S. economy into a fully socialist economy as it removed the free market concept altogether which is based on supply and demand. Thus, the U.S. was a fully socialist nation under Nixon during this period. The excerpt shows just how dire the economic outlook was at the time.

"During the 1960s, the primary goal of economic policy was to encourage growth and keep unemployment low. But by the early 1970s, the economy started to suffer from stagnation, high unemployment, and inflation, coupled with stagnant economic growth. This presented economic policymakers with a new and perplexing dilemma since unemployment and inflation usually do not coexist.

The problem with stagflation was the pain of its options. To attack inflation by reducing consumer purchasing power only made unemployment worse. The other choice was no better. Stimulating purchasing power and creating jobs also drove prices higher. Not surprisingly, economic policy during the 1970s was a nightmare of confusion and contradiction.

By 1971, pressures produced by the Vietnam War and federal social spending, coupled with the increase in foreign competition, pushed the inflation rate to 5 percent and unemployment to 6 percent...

President Richard Nixon responded by increasing federal budget deficits and devaluing the dollar in an attempt to stimulate the economy and to make American goods more competitive overseas. Nixon also imposed a 90-day wage and price freeze, followed by a mandatory set of wage-price guidelines, and then, by voluntary controls...

In 1974, during the first oil embargo, inflation hit 12 percent. Gerald Ford, the new president, initially attacked the problem in a traditional Republican fashion, by tightening the money supply by raising interest rates and limiting government spending. In the end, his economic program proved to be no more than a series of ineffectual wage and price guidelines monitored by the federal government. In the subsequent recession, unemployment reached 9 percent.

When Jimmy Carter took office in January 1977, unemployment had reached 7.4 percent. Carter responded with an ambitious spending program and called for the Federal Reserve (the Fed) to expand the money supply. Within two years, inflation had climbed to 13.3 percent.

With inflation getting out of hand, the Federal Reserve Board announced in 1979 that it would fight inflation by restraining the growth of the money supply. Unemployment increased, and interest rates rose to their highest levels in the nation's history. By November 1982, unemployment hit 10.8 percent, the highest since 1940. One out of every five American workers went some time without a job.

Along with high interest rates, the Carter administration adopted another weapon in the battle against stagflation: deregulation. Convinced that regulators too often protected the industries they were supposed to oversee, the Carter administration deregulated air and surface transportation and the savings and loan industry." ("Whipping Stagflation - Digital History").

B. Finishing what FDR Started- The End of the Gold Standard.

The gold standard serves to protect against inflation by pegging the value of a currency to gold. FDR was the first to enact a policy suspending the gold standard in 1933, after he had pushed legislation through that allowed him to do so via the Emergency Banking Act.

"In March 1933, the Emergency Banking Act gave the president the power to control international and domestic gold movements. It also gave the secretary of the treasury the power to compel surrender of gold coins and certificates. The administration waited before employing these powers, in hope that the situation would correct itself, but gold outflows continued.

On April 20, President Roosevelt issued a proclamation that formally suspended the gold standard. The proclamation prohibited exports of gold and prohibited the Treasury and financial institutions from converting currency and deposits into gold coins and ingots. The actions halted gold outflows.

In May 1933, the administration once again weakened links to gold. The Thomas amendment to the Agricultural Relief Act gave to the president the power to reduce the gold content of the dollar by as much as 50 percent. The president also received the power to back the dollar with silver, rather than gold, or with both silver and gold, at silver prices determined by the administration." (Richardson et al.).

Thus, Nixon simply finished what his Comrade in Chief had started years before. He claimed that devaluing the dollar would help to combat stagflation. The unique economic crisis was in full swing that provided Nixon the perfect cover to allow him to do something extreme but without being questioned by the public. He took the dollar off the gold standard in 1971 and the U.S. dollar was no longer convertible into gold.

As we will see in the next subsection, this policy also failed, precisely as it was designed to do. It permanently weakened the nation's currency as a result. This part of Russia and China's plan, that Nixon had carried out, was likely in anticipation of the birth of the future BRICS alliance and its gold backed currency:

"After tossing around a few bad ideas, the BRICS countries have settled on using gold as the basis for international exchange, a role previously taken by dollars and euros. This does not mean today's floating fiat ruble, real, or rand is going anywhere soon. Rather, just as the US dollar was used alongside those domestic currencies in the past, today and in the future gold will be more commonly used." (Lewis).

We will cover BRICS more in depth in the next chapter.

C. Aftereffects of Nixon's Economic Policies.

This excerpt from Investopedia shows that Nixon's policies were in fact the reason that the stagflation existed in the first place. A successful smoke screen to further the agenda of communist superpowers.

"Aftereffects of Nixon Shock

"Initially, Nixon's economic policies were widely praised as a political success. Today, however, their long-term benefits are a matter of scholarly debate.

First, the policies were the primary catalyst for the stagflation of the 1970s. They also led to the instability of floating currencies, as the U.S. dollar sank by a third during the 1970s. Over the past 40 years, the U.S. dollar has been anything but stable, with several periods of severe volatility.

From 1985 to 1995, for example, the U.S. dollar value index lost as much as 34%. After quickly recovering, it fell sharply again from 2002 to mid-2011.5

Nixon also promised that his move would prevent costly recessions. Over the past few decades, however, the U.S. has suffered severe recessions including the Great Recession of December 2007 to June 2009." (Kenton and Kelly).

4. Colombia Economist Says that Nixon Embraced Socialist Policies the Most Since FDR-

The following extract provides a clear firsthand account of American socialism under Former President Nixon. It is originally from a 1971 article published by a right-leaning libertarian think tank and Austrian school of economics called the Mises Institute. I think it is important to include the text here because not only is the piece by a Colombia educated economist and specialist in politics, but also because the piece helps remove the thick lens of party bias that still plagues many Americans. The article is from a time when America was not nearly as divided based on party lines and it gives an educated opinion on the government during that time.

"In the 1968 campaign, anarcho-Nixonism redoubled in intensity, and we were assured that Nixon was surrounded by assorted Randians, libertarians, and free-market folk straining at the leash to put their principles into action.

Well, we have had two years of Nixonism, and what we are undergoing is a super–Great Society—in fact, what we are seeing is the greatest single thrust toward socialism since the days of Franklin Roosevelt. It is not Marxian socialism, to be sure, but neither was FDR's; it is, as J.K. Galbraith wittily pointed out in New York (Sept. 21) a big-business socialism, or state corporatism, but that is cold comfort indeed.

There are only two major differences in *content* between Nixon and Kennedy-Johnson (setting aside purely stylistic differences between uptight WASP, earthy Texan, and glittering upper-class Bostonian): (1) that the march into socialism is faster because the teeth of conservative Republican opposition have been drawn; and (2) that the erstwhile "free-market" conservatives, basking in the seats of Power, have betrayed whatever principles they may have had for the service of the State.

Thus, we have Paul McCracken and Arthur F. Burns, dedicated opponents of wage-price "guideline" dictation and wage-price controls when *out* of power, now moving rapidly in the very direction they had previously deplored.

And *National Review,* acidulous opponent of the march toward statism under the Democrats, happily goes along with an even more rapid forced march under their friends the Republicans." (Rothbard).

I can only imagine what Rothbard might say regarding Nixon if he had access to the information that we have now. I commend Rothbard's article because he recognized what was taking place under not just Nixon but also other contemporary presidents including FDR. This primary source is a rarity because most Americans either didn't seem to notice the government's agenda or didn't care to look during the time. The article further corroborates that the arrogation process had been and was in process in 1971.

5. Nixon Ended the FBI Task Force that was Investigating the American Communist Party Communications with Moscow and Beijing in 1971-

Excerpt from the FBI Vault:

"COINTELPRO

The FBI began COINTELPRO—short for Counterintelligence Program—in 1956 to disrupt the activities of the Communist Party of the United States. In the 1960s, it was expanded to include a number of other domestic groups, such as the Ku

Klux Klan, the Socialist Workers Party, and the Black Panther Party. All COINTELPRO operations were ended in 1971. Although limited in scope (about two-tenths of one percent of the FBI's workload over a 15-year period), COINTELPRO was later rightfully criticized by Congress and the American people for abridging first amendment rights and for other reasons." ("COINTELPRO").

6. Antisemitic Flavored Pro-Russian Remarks from Nixon-

In the typical communist fashion, Nixon was recorded making strongly antisemitic and racist remarks. Kissinger, an antisemitic Jew, was much like Marx in this way.

"[In 1973] Nixon and Mr. Kissinger were brutally dismissive in response to requests that the United States press the Soviet Union to permit Jews to emigrate and escape persecution there.

"The emigration of Jews from the Soviet Union is not an objective of American foreign policy," Mr. Kissinger said. "And if they put Jews into gas chambers in the Soviet Union, it is not an American concern. Maybe a humanitarian concern."

"I know," Nixon responded. "We can't blow up the world because of it." (Weiss).

Later in the tape, Nixon stated:

"What it is, is it's the insecurity," he said. "It's the latent insecurity. Most Jewish people are insecure. And that's why they have to prove things." (Weiss).

7. Nixon and His Short Retirement, Then Return to Politics- After first losing to Kennedy, then the race for California governor, Nixon stated that he was retiring from politics. He then moved to New York and worked for the prominent law firm Mudge Rose Guthrie Alexander & Ferdon. The same firm would later hire a Chinese national named Gao Xiqing. Gao was born during the Mao era, and he, like Nixon, also attended Duke law school. ("Duke Law Magazine - Spanning the Continents"). Gao went on to become the President and CEO of China's largest sovereign wealth fund, the China Investment Corporation.

There is strong evidence of a considerable communist presence at Duke University's Law School. An article published by the Duke Law Journal in 1965 focuses on the rights of Communist Party members in the United States. (The Status of Anti-Communist Legislation, 1965). Duke University also established a branch in China in 2011 and is a partner of Wuhan University as of July 2023 (Knox). I don't believe I need to elaborate on Wuhan University any further. Additionally, during the Soviet era Duke Law School had at least two Polish born faculty members.

The first, Dr. Kazimierz Grzybowski began at Duke in 1964 and was an expert in Soviet Law. He authored many books on the subject. One of these was *Grzybowski: Soviet Legal Institutions: Doctrines and Social Functions.* Isaac Shapiro, a New York attorney, writes in a review of the book "He rejects the notion that Soviet social institutions are qualitatively different from the institutions of the modern welfare state in the free world, finding that Soviet institutions have remained copies of their counterparts in Western Europe." (Shapiro, 1963). The second, Dr. Wladyslaw W. Kulski, taught political science from 1964-1973.

However, socialism and communism began at Duke well
before either Professor began their tenure. "In October 1929,
students organized to form the Duke Liberal Club described
in *The Chronicle* as a forum for the discussion of economic,
social, political, and ethical problems.[1] According to Duke
historian, Robert Durden, the Liberal Club represented "a
small minority of students on campus who sympathized,
however vaguely, with the idea of social change, [and], dared
to deal critically with the subject of race relations,"[2] through
their campus discussion series. Roughly 50 students attended
the first Liberal Club meeting, and the group consisted of
about 20 members. The Liberal Club, albeit small, remained
fairly active between 1929 and 1934." ("Liberal Club"). Duke's
website link on the Liberal Club includes an image of the May
1932 edition of the "American Marxist magazine [that was]
available on the Liberal Club's library shelf" *Id.*

Nixon likely first became interested in socialism during his
time at Duke law school. Mudge Rose Guthrie Alexander &
Ferdon apparently had a pattern of hiring Duke University
alumni, another of their employees they had hired was Duke
graduate B. Leigh Kosnik. Nixon remained at Mudge for a
handful of years then returned to run for election once again.

I believe after becoming interested in socialism at Duke,
Nixon was recruited as a Soviet asset during his time at
Mudge Rose. Again, Roger Stone has publicly stated that the
mafia funded his campaign. I believe that in exchange for
Russian funding, Nixon agreed to carry out the communist
agenda once he was in office. As we are very much aware,
Russian election meddling is well documented.

8. Nixon wanted to Normalize Relations between Russia, China, and America- Nixon was the first president to visit Moscow and China and the second after FDR to visit the Soviet Union. Both visits took place after he began withdrawing U.S. troops from Vietnam and both with Henry Kissinger at his side.

A. On Nixon's China Visit and Meeting Mao Zedong from the Wilson Center:

"On the morning of February 21, 1972, US President Richard Nixon landed in the People's Republic of China.

The visit was a visual spectacle for the US President, his entourage, and much of the rest of the world, which closely watched the American leader's travels inside the world's largest communist country.

A whirlwind tour through three of China's major cities brought Nixon to several famed historical sites and cultural performances (including a revolutionary ballet), and face-to-face with many senior Chinese leaders. Photographs of Nixon standing on top the Great Wall, viewing *The Red Detachment of Women*, or toasting Chinese Premier Zhou Enlai circulated widely around the globe. So too did photos of first lady Pat Nixon inspecting a kitchen at a Beijing hotel.

Nixon's visit was not only symbolic; it was also substantive. It was a stunning development in international politics, one that has often been hailed as a "week that changed the world."

Nixon was the first American president to ever visit mainland China while in office, a now almost routine act undertaken by US heads of state. The visit helped to break several decades of US-PRC hostility and launched a new cooperative course in the relationship that generally persisted until the end of the Cold War, if not longer. The US-China rapprochement, symbolized by Nixon's visit, substantially altered the international balance of power and arguably concluded the Cold War in East Asia.

Although Nixon met with Chairman Mao Zedong only once during the visit, the two had a meaningful dialogue". (Krauss).

B. On Nixon's Moscow Visit:

"On May 22, 1972, President Richard Nixon arrives in Moscow for a summit with Soviet leaders.

Although it was Nixon's first visit to the Soviet Union as president, he had visited Moscow once before–as U.S. vice president. As Eisenhower's vice president, Nixon made frequent official trips abroad, including a 1959 trip to Moscow to tour the Soviet capital and to attend the U.S. Trade and Cultural Fair in Sokolniki Park. Soon after Vice President Nixon arrived in July 1959, he opened an informal debate with Soviet leader Nikita Khrushchev about the merits and disadvantages of their governments' political and economic systems." ("President Nixon Arrives in Moscow for Historic Summit").

9. Kissinger: Mao Zedong on an American Social Revolution, Nixon, and America's "Great Storm"-

The excerpt below is from a memo compiled by Kissinger's staff and sent to Nixon to prepare him for his upcoming visit to China. The excerpt was taken from the Department of State and shows that Mao liked Nixon and his administration. It also shows that Mao mentions an American "social revolution", that Nixon's administration was the best to approach, and that America was on the eve of a great storm. Further, Mao stated that how that storm would develop was up to the visiting students. These statements seem to be foreshadowing of something. I believe of the long-term communist control spoke of by the KGB spy in the interview. Or, perhaps, it was a code Kissinger was sending to Nixon regarding Vietnam or even Nixon's economic policies.

"Chou En-lai told an American student group that visited China in July 1971:

"In recent years Chairman Mao himself has paid attention to the American situation and he has also asked us all to note the fact that it can be said that the United States is now on the eve of a great storm. The question of how this storm develops, however, is your task, not ours. We can only tell you something of our hopes...

Mao and Chou have indicated as well, however, that any anticipated social revolution in American is a long-term prospect. They realize China's immediate concerns can be dealt with most effectively through contacts with your Administration. They are sensitive enough to the American political scene to realize that your trip to China is likely to be a positive benefit to your leadership. Mao and Chou have both observed to foreign visitors that they see your visit in relation to the 1972 Presidential campaign. They feel there is popular pressure in the U.S. for an improvement in Sino-

American relations, and they see you motivated in part by a desire to respond to those pressures in order to win re-election. By extending to you an invitation to visit their country, they evidently view the prospect of your re-election as both likely and favorable to their interests. Mao Tse-tung is reported to have remarked:

""Bad things can change into good things, and bad persons can become good persons. I like a person such as Nixon, but I do not like Social Democrats or Revisionists. These kinds of people say one thing and do another. Although Nixon has his cunning side, he is not as bad as the others, for his policy is more open." ("Foreign Relations, 1969-1976, Volume E-13, Documents on China, 1969-1972").

10. Son of American Communist Party Founder Donated $100,000 to Nixon's Campaign Fund and Illegally Donated to Watergate Fund-

"WASHINGTON, Oct. 1—Armand Hammer, the millionaire oilman and art collector who pioneered in United States-Soviet trade, pleaded guilty in Federal District Court today to three misdemeanor charges of making illegal contributions in the names of other persons to the 1972 Nixon re-election campaign.

Dr. Hammer also admitted that he subsequently, concealed the illegal contributions, which totaled $54,000, by lying to the Senate Watergate committee and by agreeing to use yet another person as the "fictitious source" of the funds—an agreement that led to the execution of a "sham promissory note" to that person. These acts were not essential elements of the three misdemeanors to which Dr. Hammer pleaded.

However, the special Watergate prosecutor apparently insisted on Dr. Hammer's admission as a condition of a plea bargain." (Oelsner).

11. Kissinger's Secret Trip to China in 1971- This secret trip made by Kissinger at Nixon's urging is likely where the instruction came from China that Nixon should take the dollar off the gold standard. According to the US-China Institute, Kissinger was in China from July 9th through the 11th. Nixon officially made the announcement regarding the end of the gold standard the following month.

"A documentary history of US efforts under Richard Nixon to open discussions with Chinese leaders, an effort that yielded Kissinger's trip forty years ago this month. Photo: Premier Zhou Enlai and National Security Advisor Henry Kissinger." ("Getting to Beijing: Henry Kissinger's Secret 1971 Trip | US-China Institute").

Conclusion

This chapter has covered a great deal of evidence regarding Nixon's communist agenda and his role in aiding the arrogation of the United States. It has examined Nixon's immediate withdrawal of U.S. troops from Vietnam in his first year of office, his severed agreement with South Vietnam, and his 1968 intentional sabotage of the Vietnamese peace accord to win office and further the communists' plans. We have also examined his devastating economic policies, which continue to negatively affect the U.S. economy and improve those of our enemies. There have been many strong indicators of the arrogation process that we have seen throughout the evidence presented and how Nixon enabled each one. Next, we will cover some modern evidence proving that arrogation is not only still currently underway but nearing completion.

TEN

Chapter 10: Evidence III: Today

I   ntroduction

This chapter will not include the same amount of circumstantial evidence as the two prior chapters. Not only because we have already established that our nation now lies somewhere between a social democracy and a democratic socialist state since FDR, but also because it would simply be too much to list. My focus for this book is to spread a serious yet grievous message to my fellow Christians and Americans. I feel that I have already included enough evidence to prove that the message is a valid one.

For those who may argue that the large list of evidence included in this work are merely coincidences, I urge them to get more familiar with the definition of coincidence under probability and the types of casual connections that govern them. They will find that the word "coincidence" does not describe what I have put forward. The casual connection between the evidence is the arrogation of our nation by leaders who either shared or share socialist ideology or simply furthered the goal of socialist powers for money. Then there are those who anticipated the rise of the East. These would've wanted to ensure that they and their families were on the side of China and Russia when America is hardly a top three nation in terms of GDP ("The World in 2050") and the top ten positions are dominated by hostile nations to the West. Whatever their reasoning, they are traitors to the United States.

Moving on, this chapter will primarily focus on the Biden and Obama administrations and on California and New York, two of the three states with the largest GDPs in the nation. Until 2006, New York and California were at the top of the list of the largest GDPs. However, these states have steadily declined in many aspects over the last few decades, and the reasons behind that decline are clear: to bring about the economic decline of the U.S. by China and Russia. Our economic decline is crucial to help weaken any resistance during the final steps of arrogation. Just as was seen in the Great Depression, the stagnation of the 1970s, and the Great Recession of 2008, the more worn down that we are, the easier we will comply with the implementation of communist policies.

Alas, we will now examine some pieces of modern-day evidence showing that we are now living during the final steps of arrogation. As we have seen, a leader from either the Republican Party or the Democratic Party may be in office to see the process to its completion. Again, our enemies are not at all concerned with America's political parties, but only with the politicians they can use. China and Russia, of course, like to use our party system to their benefit by dividing and further weakening our population.

The final policies as we near completion will likely resemble those found in China and Russia today: inescapable surveillance, rewards for those who turn in "enemies of the state' among family and friends, a digital economy, socialist indoctrination, loss of private property, and strict control. All of these heavily reflect policies that we can expect the Antichrist to make full use of. Thus, they are not inherently surprising.

Biden, Obama, China, and Socialism

It is important to keep in mind that our current Commander in Chief was also a part of the socialist policies that China-backed Former President Obama instituted during the Great Recession. Like all socialist policies, they allowed more government control of the economy.

A. Chinese Funding for Obama's 2012 Campaign.

A Reuters article covered Leonardo Di Caprio's testimony in court where the movie star stated that Jho Low told him he supported the Democratic Party and planned to donate between $20 and $30 million dollars to help get Obama reelected as president. Jho Low is a Malaysian national of Chinese heritage and there were several reports that China helped harbor Low. This timeline is exceedingly important because Xi took power in 2013, just a year after Obama's second term. Further, many of Low's deals concerned China's belt and road initiative which Obama willfully ignored allowing for China to build up its global web of influence.

"Actor Leonardo DiCaprio told a Washington jury on Monday that Malaysian financier Jho Low revealed his plans to donate up to $30 million to help U.S. President Barack Obama's 2012 reelection campaign in what prosecutors allege was part of an illegal foreign influence operation.

"It was a casual conversation about what party he was in support of," DiCaprio said, telling jurors that Low said he planned on giving "a significant donation" to the Democratic Party that was "somewhere to the tune of $20-30 million." (Lynch).

The willful refusal of Obama to focus on building relationships in South and Central America, especially during the 2013 launch of Xi's belt and road initiative (BRI), has allowed for a host of Chinese and Russian aligned nations to be parked on our doorstep. If they chose to, Russia or China could launch an attack from Cuba, Venezuela, or others at any given time. Both nations and many others in the region are now a part of BRI. In short, Obama contributed heavily to the U.S. being surrounded by communist enemies. Considering the year that BRI began, and keeping in mind Xi's rise to power, it is blatantly obvious why Low was willing to donate so much money to ensure Obama's 2012 victory.

B. Obamanomics.

Excerpt from Investopedia:

"Critics of Obamanomics view it as representing an undue expansion of the government's economic role, including increased government spending, taxation, and regulation....

To detractors, the term Obamanomics has connotations of increased government spending, taxation, and regulation, and a dangerous slide toward socialism and a command economy." (Fernando).

C. Bidenomics.

Biden's policies are damaging some of the few remaining free market qualities left in our economy. In so doing, he is tilting it more toward a socialist economy instead of mixed. Excerpt from The Hill:

"Deng Xiaoping, who led China from 1978-89, famously described his effort to integrate limited, free market capitalism into China's communist system as "socialism with Chinese characteristics." Taking that step helped China become an economic powerhouse and the world's second largest economy.

Chinese President Xi Jinping has been steadily undoing Deng's reforms by imposing top-down, command-and-control policies, and China is suffering for it both economically and politically. Ironically, President Joe Biden has been abandoning the U.S. version of free market capitalism that Deng admired and increasingly embracing variations of Xi's policies. Call it Xinomics with American characteristics." (Mathews).

D. Moving Closer to Socialism, too Much Even for Democratic Socialists.

An excerpt from Politico, an independent political news agency on Biden's socialist policies:

"There may be deep divisions within the Republican universe these days — over trade, Ukraine, Trump, Fox News — but there's one unifying assertion: President Joe Biden is hell-bent on taking the United States down the road to socialism." (Greenfield).

Apparently, Biden is proving to be too socialist even for the Democratic Socialists of America Party. The following comes from the World Socialist Organization's website. The website delivers socialist news across the world, which makes the article much less biased against the left, and that much more shocking:

"The Democratic Socialists of America (DSA) is preparing to move further to the right as the Biden administration and the Democratic-controlled Congress unabashedly prosecute the interests of Wall Street and American imperialism and reject even the paltriest proposals for social reform." (London).

California

A. Following the Money.

We have already established that the Russian mafia operate under the control of the FSB and oftentimes they are one and the same. Moving back to the article on Russian organized crime discussed in Chapter 6 by the Federation of American Scientists, the most surprising points discussed was the movement of money. The Russian mafia, or rather, the FSB acting as the Russian mafia, moved vast sums of money derived through their criminal activities not from the U.S. to European or Russian accounts, but from Russia and Europe to U.S. accounts.

"Russian organized crime groups in the former Soviet Union are wire transferring huge amounts of money, ranging from several thousand to millions of dollars from bank accounts located in Finland, Cayman Islands, and Europe to U.S. banks.", "The source of this money is believed to come from narcotics activity, illegal trade in arms and antiques, and prostitution. Money is also stolen from the Russian government. According to a Russian newspaper, upwards of 1.5 trillion rubles (worth in excess of $1 billion) were stolen from the state with forged documents in 1992 to 1993." (Russian Organized Criminal Activities in California). The article states that the funds were placed in banks in both L.A. and San Francisco.

Moving money, especially money "stolen" from the Russian government into U.S. accounts is particularly strange for several reasons. First, because even in the 1990s, America had considerably strict banking controls. It would've been difficult for a Russian national to open a bank account, at least when compared to a U.S. citizen, due to the aggressive American attitude toward the Soviet Union. Also, such large sums would've drawn a great deal of suspicion and attention likely from state and federal law enforcement.

Third, with the FSB keeping a relentlessly tight grip on the Russian mafia, it is virtually impossible to think that they could have stolen any amount from the Russian government, much less the equivalent of $1 billion dollars. In addition, faking documents that would pass muster would have not been likely either. The Russian government would have undoubtedly known about and sanctioned the transfers.

In this case, the Russia mafia, or rather the FSB, would have had to have been working with corrupt U.S. or California government officials to not have immediately raised red flags and been investigated. There would've needed to have been powerful people at play working behind the scenes. Likely, the very same people loyal to the Kremlin who would have been collecting payments from Russia.

I would venture a guess that a large portion of the payments were going to the communists in the film industry. It is after all well known to implement thought patterns in the masses via television programs and movies. This would coincide with some of the banks that held the Russian funds being located in L.A. An additional anomaly is that at the time of the article, there was no U.S. intelligence data relating to the Russian mafia "Because there is a lack of intelligence data relating to Russian organized crime groups and their structure in this country, it is almost impossible at the present time to determine their magnitude or scope of operations. Based upon this lack of information, it is difficult to develop efficient strategies to counter them" (Russian Organized Criminal Activities in California).

B. The Chinese Lab.

An unlicensed Chinese lab was somehow able to exist directly in the heart of California. Its operators were able to collect continuous payments from the People's Republic of China (PRC), conduct experiments, obtain some of the most dangerous pathogens in the world, and mice capable of transmitting those pathogens. Considering the lab's outrageous activities, it is unfathomable to think that somewhere in the California or the federal government there was not individuals who were aware of the lab's existence. In fact, common sense would point to the lab having help from corrupt officials loyal to the PRC to remain active and hidden.

"Here's what the Committee found:

·   The illegal biolab was run by a PRC citizen who is a wanted fugitive from Canada with a $330 million Canadian dollar judgment against him for stealing American intellectual property.

·   This PRC citizen was a top official at a PRC-state-controlled company and had links to military-civil fusion entities.

·   The illegal biolab received millions of dollars in unexplained payments from PRC banks while running the illegal biolab.

·   The illegal biolab contained thousands of samples of labeled, unlabeled, and encoded potential pathogens, including HIV, malaria, tuberculosis, and Covid.

·   The illegal biolab also contained a freezer labeled "Ebola," which contained unlabeled, sealed silver bags consistent with how the lab stored high risk biological materials. Ebola is a Select Agent with a lethality rate between 25-90%.

·   The biolab contained nearly a thousand transgenic mice, genetically engineered to mimic the human immune system. Lab workers said that the mice were designed "to catch and carry the COVID-19 virus."

·   After local officials who discovered the lab sought help from the CDC and others, the CDC refused to test any of the samples." ("Select Committee Unveils Report on Illegal PRC-Tied Biolab in Reedley, CA with McCarthy & Costa").

C. Governor Gavin Newsome. Governor Newsome has maintained an excellent relationship with Xi Jinping and China. Late in 2023, he went to China and met with Xi. Newsome is the first governor to meet with Xi in nearly a decade. The following extract is from the official website of the governor.

"Governor Newsom met with Chinese President Xi Jinping and other high-level Chinese officials to discuss climate action, economic development, cultural exchange, human rights concerns, and democracy.

BEIJING – On Wednesday, Governor Gavin Newsom met with President Xi Jinping in China's capital city of Beijing. The Governor also met Wednesday with Foreign Minister Wang Yi and Vice President Han Zheng and signed a new climate-focused Memorandum of Understanding (MOU) with the National Development and Reform Commission Chairman Zheng Shanjie. The Governor was joined by U.S. Ambassador to China Nicholas Burns for the series of discussions.

Governor Newsom was the first governor to be in China in more than four years, and the first to meet with President Xi since former Governor Brown in 2017." ("Governor Newsom Meets with Chinese President Xi Jinping").

Uncoincidentally, Newsome also met with Canadian Prime Minister Justin Trudeau who is notoriously Pro-China. The two gladly embraced Xi in San Francisco late last year. Naturally, he and Trudeau agreed to keep in contact.

"Today, Prime Minister Justin Trudeau met with the Governor of California, Gavin Newsom, on the margins of the Asia-Pacific Economic Cooperation (APEC) Leaders' Summit in San Francisco, United States of America.

The Prime Minister and the Governor discussed their shared commitment to fighting climate change while growing strong economies and making life more affordable for the middle class. As part of this work, they discussed ongoing collaboration under the *Climate action and nature protection: Memorandum of co-operation between Canada and California*, signed in 2022 on the margins of the Summit of the Americas. Canada and California continue to work together on electric vehicles, and the Prime Minister and the Governor discussed opportunities on clean energy, including resilient clean electricity grids, nuclear energy, and carbon capture, utilization, and storage.

With Canada and California as recognized leaders on innovation, the Prime Minister and the Governor exchanged views on artificial intelligence, as well as support for journalism and its role in strong, healthy democracies. They also discussed continued collaboration on trade and agriculture, to support workers and consumers on both sides of the border.

The Prime Minister and the Governor agreed to remain in contact and looked forward to further collaboration on issues of importance to Canadians and Californians alike." ("Prime Minister Justin Trudeau Meets with Governor of California Gavin Newsom").

New York

A. Chinese police station in New York. Chinese agents opened a police station in Brooklyn, New York City. The agents were working with around three dozen officers from the China's national police force who were harassing dissidents inside America by using social media. It was one of three cases being prosecuted last year by the Justice Department. However, before being arrested, the agents had learned of the FBI investigation and deleted communications from their phones. The tip off confirms that there are in fact active China loyalists within the FBI or elsewhere in the federal executive branch.

"The cases are part of a series of Justice Department prosecutions in recent years aimed at disrupting Chinese government efforts to locate in America pro-democracy activists and others who are openly critical of Beijing's policies and to suppress their speech.

One of three cases announced Monday concerns a local branch of the Chinese Ministry of Public Security that had operated inside an office building in Manhattan's Chinatown neighborhood before closing last fall amid an FBI investigation. The two men who were arrested were acting under the direction and control of a Chinese government official and deleted communication with that official from their phones after learning of the FBI's probe in an apparent effort to obstruct the inquiry, according to the Justice Department." (NEUMEISTER and TUCKER).

As with the Chinese Lab in Fresno, it is highly unlikely that the Chinese police would be able to set up an active office in New York without coordinating with individuals within the U.S. government. The Director of the F.B.I. apparently agrees:

"I have to be careful about discussing our specific investigative work, but to me, it's outrageous to think that the Chinese police would attempt to set up shop in New York, for example, without proper coordination," the FBI director said...

While tasked with cracking down on Chinese-related illegal activities overseas, the police stations represent "the latest iteration in [China's] growing transnational repression, where it seeks to police and limit political expression far beyond its own borders," the report said." (Farivar).

B. Governor Kathy Hochel. Governor Kathy Hochel of New York is friends with Chinese Official Huang Ping, the Consul General in New York. She met with him in 2019 when she served as the Lieutenant Governor. Ping has claimed that human rights abuses in China are false, promotes a Chinese invasion of Taiwan, and has described the Chinese Communist Party as being a party focused on the global common good (Cawthorne).

Hochel regularly celebrates the Chinese Lunar New Year by attending the China Town Parade. This year, she was joined by Huang Ping, New York Mayor Eric Adams, and U.S. Senator

Chuck Schumer. She is also a supporter of China-U.S. relations. (Joseph).

"I look forward to continuing to strengthen our culture, social, and economic ties in the future," Hochul said in a letter written for an event promoting U.S.-China relations back in November.

The CPC is known for utilizing statecraft at the local level to advance its interests. According to a report authored by the Foundation for Defense of Democracies, China "uses relationships that Beijing builds with state and local leaders as tools for advancing a strategic campaign of malign influence in the United States." (Cawthorne).

The latter part of the excerpt above is of substantial importance as all four Chinese Consulates-General and both Russian Consulates-General are in cities led by the Democratic Party. Local government officials, such as Mayors, can sign sister-city agreements which China and Russia have been known to use for espionage purposes. This practice is highlighted by an excerpt from the Washington Examiner:

"We need to take proper action and have the GAO do a deep dive into what is happening with these partnerships and these programs that are involving foreign communities in countries where we have adverse relationships," Blackburn told the *Washington Examiner* in an interview. "We should look at how we should manage these sister city partnerships, which is important for us to do to protect our nation and to protect our sovereignty." (Roth).

New York and Los Angeles currently have several sister-city agreements with cities in both China and Russia including Beijing and St. Petersburg according to sistercities.org. L.A. also has a standing agreement with Tehran.

BRICS

Former President Obama severely missed when it came to building relationships with several key nations as an attempt to dissuade them from joining the BRICS alliance. Judging from Mr. Low's very generous campaign contribution, the belt and road initiative beginning in 2013, Xi's term beginning in 2013, and Obama's refusal to inhibit BRI, I believe that the former president accomplished precisely what he intended to where BRICS is concerned. Especially considering that like Obama's first term, BRICS also first started cooperating in 2008 (Papa).

Recall that both FDR and Nixon ensured that the U.S. dollar is no longer backed by gold. BRICS, not by coincidence, decided to use gold to back its currency. As you might have suspected, both China and Russia have been the largest gold buyers in the last 20 years (Parker). But essentially all BRICS nations were at the top of the chart of nations buying gold between 2017-2022:

"Other countries whose relations with the U.S. may be worsening have also purchased gold. From 2017 to 2022, the central banks of Russia, Turkey, India, and China were the largest buyers of gold.

And while Russia, Turkey, India, and China account for nearly 60% of the net change in gold reserves globally from 2017 to

2022, it is small countries in the Middle East and North Africa that are buying gold at the fastest rates." (Comen).

In short, Obama provided Xi Jinping with yet another major route that he could use to damage the U.S. dollar and alienate our nation from several of its most important allies. Among these are India and Brazil. Further still, Biden has yet to even develop a BRICS policy much less act on it (Papa). All the while, BRICS continues to expand and now includes Iran, Saudi Arabia, Egypt, UAE, and Ethiopia.

"BRICS is a formidable group – it accounts for 41% of the world's population, 31.5% of global gross domestic product and 16% of global trade [before its latest expansion]. As such, it has a lot of bargaining power if the countries act together – which they increasingly do. During the Ukraine war, Moscow's BRICS partners have ensured Russia's economic and diplomatic survival in the face of Western attempts to isolate Moscow. Brazil, India, China and South Africa engaged with Russia in 166 BRICS events in 2022. And some members became crucial export markets for Russia." (Papa).

Conclusion

The circumstantial evidence presented in this chapter and the prior chapters hopefully paint a detailed picture of what is happening within our nation. The arrogation of America by China and Russia has been a very long process. Unfortunately, it has involved many in our state and federal governments, and the administrative state has been used excessively for this purpose.

We do, thankfully, have a lot of officials loyal to America within our federal law enforcement agencies. We can see signs of this as communist-aligned traitors to our nation are still being arrested and prosecuted. Examples include Charles McGonigal, Aldrich Ames, Robert Hanssen, and Ana Montes. However, this is a two-edged sword as it also only further proves the existence of communist agents within our federal government.

I don't quite believe that the communist loyalists in these agencies will necessarily overpower those remaining that are loyal to America and seize leadership. Instead, I suspect that soon enough the officials who are loyal to America will one day wake up and realize who exactly it is that their supervisors are taking their orders from: China and Russia. By that time, I think that the internet and media will be so censored that the average American likewise won't realize what has happened until it is too late.

We are seeing more signs of America's takeover now as the nation and the world begin to look more unrecognizable each week. Sadly, we can expect it to only worsen with time. As we approach the arrival of the Antichrist and the Final War described in Ezekiel, the arrogation process will become more evident each day until it is complete.

ELEVEN

Chapter 11: West Becomes East

America of the East

A Alas, we will briefly cover the position of the United States during the final battle. We will also look at how the arrogation of the United States will fit into that position. I have, of course, alluded to this issue and to my view regarding it throughout this book, but I will briefly expound on my perspective once again here. In consideration of all the points and evidence covered throughout this book, I firmly believe that the United States will not be able to answer the call to aid Israel because it will no longer be the United States. Or, at least not as we currently know it.

As we have seen, the process of arrogation is already well underway. It began nearly 100 years ago with Former President Roosevelt and has since been strengthened or quickened through key presidents who were also corrupted by socialism. I believe sometime between now and the time of the Antichrist's rise, our nation will firmly be a modern communist state operating strictly under the control of Russia and China. Essentially, it will be a puppet state, much like many former Soviet satellite nations are today.

Role of AI

I firmly believe that artificial intelligence (AI) will greatly accelerate America's arrogation. AI is a tool that the Chinese Communist Party (CCP) has been using for some time to help it spy on its population and now on those of other nations. Xi and his government are known to take any tool available and use it in the most extreme way to bend the Chinese people and the world to his will.

An example of this is the CCP's recent launch of its AI-powered satellite, which it will use to gather intelligence and boost its military capabilities in a war "it is positioned over an area that includes Taiwan, the South China Sea, and other potential flashpoints. Pairing its sharp eyes with artificial intelligence (ai) and information from other satellites could give China a unique ability to keep tabs on vehicles and vessels in the region. That would come in handy in the event of war, suggests a new analysis by the Centre for Strategic and International Studies in Washington." ("China's Satellites Are Improving Rapidly. Its Army Will Benefit"). Earlier last year, Wuhan University also experimented with an AI-powered satellite. Xi Jinping knows no limits when it comes to furthering the power and control of China and its Communist Party.

We often hear in Western news that America is leading the AI race. This, however, is simply not true. Bloomberg reported late in 2023 that Chinese companies filed nearly twice the number of patents related to AI over the prior year than the U.S. did ("China Widens Lead Over US in AI Patents After Beijing Tech Drive"). China has long been a tech-oriented nation and it has a massive population. Thus, the U.S. is behind here too. Interestingly, the technology involved with AI is not new. In fact, China began to work on AI technology in the 1970s, but its origin dates back much further, even to ancient times.

I believe that artificial intelligence was the same technology used before the Great Flood and was derived from the Nephilim. There are mentions of it in both ancient Chinese and Greek writings "in the works of Homer (c. eighth century BCE), we find Hephaestus, the Greek god of smithing and craft, using automatic bellows to execute simple, repetitive labor. Golden handmaidens, endowed with the characteristics of movement, perception, judgment, and speech, assist him in his work." ("Surveillance, Companionship, and Entertainment: The Ancient History of Intelligent Machines"). We are now seeing history repeat itself once more. Just as it was in the days of Noah, it is now. We are, I believe, uncomfortably close to the period of tribulation and to the Final Battle.

What Can We do? Trust in God!

While we as Christians can do our part in at least helping to slow down the arrogation process of our once great democracy, the purpose of this book is not necessarily a call to arms. Rather, it has an informational purpose, a message that I hope was delivered. That message is for those who simply do not understand what happened to the nation they so fondly remember. Or those unaware of what exactly is going on around them but can feel that something is just not quite right.

Apart from educating others as to what the truth really is, we can slow down the socialist powers at work in our country by remaining observant and through legal means. Petitions can go a long way in the right circumstances, as can a court case against a corrupt official with some adequate evidence. Above all else, I simply recommend prayer and trust in the plan that God has for us and for the world.

I have always subscribed to the belief that God's will precedes everything else. After all, with the U.S. not being mentioned in Ezekiel 38 or 39, we can only assume that the arrogation of America is part of God's plan. It would be a requisite for Israel to stand alone against Russia and its demonic coalition of nations before being rescued by divine intervention. Still, prayer for discernment and remembering God's grand plan for us is paramount to navigate these dark days that we live in. I pray that our Heavenly Father guides us all with his light and blesses us with strength as we make our way through them.

TWELVE

Chapter 12: Disinformation

Q oshet Method

Because our "independent fact-checkers" are also highly politicized, the alignment of members from both parties with Russia and China, and the article on the KGB defector describing the Soviet's plan, I thought it salient to create a quick test we can use to help discern information that is truthful from that which is influenced. By influenced, I mean by socialists, politicians, and those with an ulterior motive.

This simple but effective test can work for either an entity, such as a company or agency, or an individual, such as a politician or CEO. Its intended purpose is to help uncover if a piece of information should be regarded as credible and can be believed based on the score of the source from which the information came from.

I have termed this method the Qoshet Method from the Hebrew קֹשְׁט † , which means truth or reality (Strong's Concordance #7189).

The method is limited to the information we have available on that person or entity, but like a chain, we can also search for more information and then examine each piece we receive about a person or entity using the same method. Thus, linking them together until we get a conclusive answer. This will allow us to determine if the information should be used to help build the score for the initial person or entity being examined or if it should simply be disregarded.

How it works

You may see an article, for example, during research and want to know if it is credible before using or sharing it. You would then find the name of the source from which the article originated and write it down on the Qoshet Method worksheet along with the year established.

Review and carefully consider a set number of relevant questions concerning the source and assign the article a score based on each question. I suggest at least 5 questions worth 20 points each.

Start with a baseline of 100 points. After answering each question, a negative score would denote that the article should not be trusted, whereas a positive score indicates that it is trustworthy and probably not influenced by politics or external actors. If the answer to a question cannot be found, assign a 0 for that question.

Example: I have completed an example using the article 39 Years Ago, a KGB Defector Chillingly Predicted Modern America (Ratner). See the following worksheet and note the score assigned to Big Think.

Qoshet Method

Questions: 5. 20 points each

Baseline: 100 points

Contamination/Suspected Influence Scale: Positive = More Trustworthy (The higher the + = more trust). Negative = less trustworthy (the lower the - = less trust). Neutral (baseline score only) = Inconclusive.

Name of Article in Issue: "39 Years Ago, a KGB Defector Chillingly Predicted Modern America".

Name of the Source: Big Think.

Year Founded: 2007.

Owned by: Freethink Media. Big Think was founded by Peter Brown and Victoria Brown according to their website.

1. Evidence of owners being influenced by politics? Relationship with Lawrence Summers, Former Treasury Secretary (D). -20.

2. Evidence of owners being influenced by external actors? None. +20.

3. Does the article theme or topic indicate influence by politics? No. It describes information damaging to both political parties. +20.

4. Does the article theme or topic indicate influence by external actors? No. It describes information damaging to external actors. +20.

5. Is the source associated with or mentioned by entities or people known to be associated with politics or external actors? The source and its owners were mentioned in an article in the New York Times. An entity very likely to be strongly associated with the Democratic Party and possibly external actors. -20.

Other Considerations that might affect score or reliability– Big Think's stated mission per its website, bigthink.com, is to produce independent information free from the toxicity of politics.

Although Summers and other very wealthy individuals with questionable motives invested in Big Think, Summers has been out of office for quite some time. Furthermore, the article in question is damaging to both major political parties and external actors. No effect on the reliability of the article.

Total: 160 points.

<u>Conclusion</u>: High positive score. The article by Big Think is very likely to be trustworthy.

References

R eferences

Abington School District v. Schempp, 374 U.S. 203 (1963).

"Al Jazeera Condemns Israeli Forces Killing of Cameraman Samer Abudaqa." *Al Jazeera*, 15 Dec. 2023, www.aljazeera.com/news/2023/12/15/al-jazeera-condemns-israeli-forces-killing-of-cameraman-samer-abu-daqqa. Accessed 12 Mar. 2024.

"A Response From Armand Hammer." *The New York Times - Breaking News, US News, World News and Videos*, 20 Dec. 1981, www.nytimes.com/1981/12/20/magazine/l-a-response-from-armand-hammer-139417.html. Accessed 7 Mar. 2024.

Richardson et al., Gary, et al. "Roosevelt's Gold Program." *Federal Reserve History*, www.federalreservehistory.org/essays/roosevelts-gold-program. Accessed 10 Mar. 2024.

Arango, Tim. "Ex-Harvard President Meets a Former Student, and Intellectual Sparks Fly." *The New York Times - Breaking News, US News, World News and Videos*, 7 Jan. 2008, www.nytimes.com/2008/01/07/technology/07summers.html. Accessed 2 Mar. 2024.

Aslund, Anders. "Why Has Russia's Economic Transformation Been So Arduous?" *Carnegie Endowment for International Peace*, 28 Apr. 1999, carnegieendowment.org/sada/201. Accessed 4 Mar. 2024.

Bearak, Max. "The U.S. Is Paying Billions to Russia's Nuclear Agency. Here's Why." *The New York Times - Breaking News, US News, World News and Videos*, 14 June 2023, www.nytimes.com/2023/06/14/climate/enriched-uranium-nuclear-russia-ohio.html. Accessed 4 Mar. 2024.

Berman, Larry. *No Peace, No Honor: Nixon, Kissinger, and Betrayal in Vietnam*. Simon & Schuster, 2001.

Bloom, S. F. (1942). Karl Marx and the Jews. *Jewish Social Studies*, 4(1), 3–16. http://www.jstor.org/stable/4615185

Breuninger, Kevin, and Eamon James. "Henry Kissinger Told White House He Talked to Xi About Trump, Kudlow Says." *CNBC*, 19 Dec. 2019, www.cnbc.com/2019/12/18/henry-kissinger-told-white-house-he-talked-to-xi-about-trump-kudlow-says.html. Accessed 10 Mar. 2024.

Burke, Jason. "Antisemitism is Deeply Ingrained in European Society, Says EU Official." *The Guardian*, 30 Oct. 2023, www.theguardian.com/news/2023/oct/30/antisemitism-deeply-ingrained-in-european-society-says-eu-official. Accessed 12 Mar. 2024.

Cawthorne, Cameron. "NY Gov. Hochul Met with Chinese Official Who Called Genocide of Uyghur Muslims 'lies'." *Fox News*, 13 Jan. 2022, www.foxnews.com/politics/new-york-hochul-met-chinese-official-genocide-uyghur-muslims-lies. Accessed 11 Mar. 2024.

Center for Strategic and International Studies. "Significant Cyber Incidents." CSIS, www.csis.org/programs/strategic-technologies-program/significant-cyber-incidents.

"CHILE: Cousin's Cinema." *TIME.com*, Time Magazine, 9 July 1934, content.time.com/time/subscriber/article/0,33009,769917,00.html. Accessed 8 Mar. 2024.

"China Widens Lead Over US in AI Patents After Beijing Tech Drive." *Bloomberg - Are You a Robot?*, 24 Oct. 2023, www.bloomberg.com/news/articles/2023-10-24/china-widens-lead-over-us-in-ai-patents-after-beijing-tech-drive?embedded-checkout=true. Accessed 12 Mar. 2024.

"China's Satellites Are Improving Rapidly. Its Army Will Benefit." *The Economist*, 7 Mar. 2024, www.economist.com/china/2024/03/07/chinas-satellites-are-improving-rapidly-the-pla-will-benefit.   Accessed 12 Mar. 2024.

Church of the Holy Trinity v. United States, 143 U.S. 457 (1892).

Coalson, Robert. "Seeing Red: Russia's Communist Party Makes Gains In New Duma, But Does It Matter?" *RadioFreeEurope/RadioLiberty*, 22 Sept. 2021, www.rferl.org/a/russia-communist-Party-duma/31473164.html. Accessed 4 Mar. 2024.

"COINTELPRO." *FBI.gov*, vault.fbi.gov/cointel-pro. Accessed 10 Mar. 2024.

Comen, Evan. "These Countries Are Buying up the World's Gold." *24/7 Wall Street*, 6 Aug. 2023, 247wallst.com/special-report/2023/08/06/countries-buying-up-the-worlds-gold/. Accessed 11 Mar. 2024.

"Consulate General of the People's Republic of China in San Francisco."   , sanfrancisco.china-consulate.gov.cn/eng/. Accessed 11 Mar. 2024.

Crews Jr., Clyde W. "How Many Rules And Regulations Do Federal Agencies Issue?" *Forbes*, 15 Aug. 2017, www.forbes.com/sites/waynecrews/2017/08/15/how-many-rules-and-regulations-do-federal-agencies-issue/?sh=5b718d141e64. Accessed 3 Mar. 2024.

Darrien, cook. The new right: a journey to the fringes of American Politics. New York, NY: All Points Books, 2019. Print.

Dunlop, Dale. "Campobello - Franklin Roosevelt's Second Home." *The Maritime Explorer*, 1 Aug. 2021, themaritimeexplorer.ca/2021/08/01/campobello/. Accessed 8 Mar. 2024.

"Duke Law Magazine - Spanning the Continents." *Duke University School of Law*, 1986, web.law.duke.edu/news/pdf/lawmagwinter86.pdf. Accessed 11 Mar. 2024.

"Direct Evidence." Legal Information Institute, Cornell Law School, https://www.law.cornell.edu/wex/circumstantial_evidence. Accessed 3 Mar. 2024.

"Ending the Vietnam War, 1969–1973." *Office of the Historian*, history.state.gov/milestones/1969-1976/ending-vietnam. Accessed 10 Mar. 2024.

"European Jewish groups call for better security." *Times of Israel*, 17 Sept. 2014, www.timesofisrael.com/european-jewish-groups-call-for-security-fight-against-anti-semitism/. Accessed 12 Mar. 2024.

Farivar, Masood. "FBI Investigating Chinese 'Police Station' In New York." *Voice of America*, 18 Nov. 2022, www.voanews.com/a/fbi-investigating-chinese-police-station-in-new-york/6839791.html. Accessed 11 Mar. 2024.

"FDR's Alphabet Soup." *US History*, www.ushistory.org/us/49e.asp. Accessed 7 Mar. 2024.

Fentanyl Flow to the United States. DEA Intelligence Report, 2020, www.dea.gov/sites/default/files/2020-03/DEA_GOV_DIR-008-20%20Fentanyl%20Flow%20in%20the%20United%20States_0.pdf. Accessed 15 Mar. 2024.

Fernando, Jason. "Obamanomics: What It Means, How It Works." *Investopedia*, 1 Sept. 2021, www.investopedia.com/terms/o/obamanomics.asp. Accessed 11 Mar. 2024.

"Foreign Relations of the United States: Diplomatic Papers, 1944, China, Volume VI." *Office of the Historian*, history.state.gov/historicaldocuments/frus1944v06/d453. Accessed 9 Mar. 2024.

"Foreign Relations, 1969-1976, Volume E-13, Documents on China, 1969-1972." *U.S. Department of State Archive*, 1 Feb. 1971, 2001-2009.state.gov/r/pa/ho/frus/nixon/e13/72537.htm. Accessed 10 Mar. 2024.

Friedman, George, and Meredith Friedman. *The Future of War: Power, Technology and American World Dominance in the Twenty-First Century.* 2002.

"Getting to Beijing: Henry Kissinger's Secret 1971 Trip | US-China Institute." *US-China Institute* |, 21 July 2011, china.usc.edu/getting-beijing-henry-kissingers-secret-1971-trip. Accessed 10 Mar. 2024.

"Governor Newsom Meets with Chinese President Xi Jinping." *California Governor*, 25 Oct. 2023, www.gov.ca.gov/2023/10/25/governor-newsom-meets-with-chinese-president-xi-jinping/. Accessed 11 Mar. 2024.

Greenfield, Jeff. "Joe Biden, Scandinavian." *Politico*, 14 Mar. 2023, www.politico.com/news/magazine/2023/03/14/biden-stealth-socialist-opinion-00086781. Accessed 11 Mar. 2024.

Hines, Nico. "Why the NSA Told Henry Kissinger to Drop Dead When He Tried to Cut Intel Links with Britain." *The Daily Beast*, 23 Oct. 2020, www.thedailybeast.com/why-the-nsa-told-henry-kissinger-to-drop-dead-when-he-tried-to-cut-intel-links-with-britain. Accessed 10 Mar. 2024.

"How Courts Work." *American Bar Association*, 9 Sept. 2019, www.americanbar.org/groups/public_education/resources/law_related_ Accessed 6 Mar. 2024.

Huntington, Samuel. Who are we? Challenges to America's national identity. New York: Simon & Schuster Paperbacks, 2004. Print.

Ignatius, David. *The Washington Post*, 4 May 2021, www.washingtonpost.com/opinions/2021/05/04/russias-plot-control-internet-is-no-longer-secret/. Accessed 4 Mar. 2024.

"IMF Datamapper - MAP (2024)." www.imf.org/external/datamapper/. Accessed 6 Mar. 2024.

Joseph, Jamie. "Huang Ping, 'purveyor of CCP Propaganda,' Joins Schumer, Top New York Dems at Chinese New Year Parade." *Fox News*, 27 Feb. 2024, www.foxnews.com/politics/huang-ping-purveyor-ccp-propaganda-joins-schumer-top-new-york-dems-chinese-new-year-parade. Accessed 11 Mar. 2024.

Isaac Shapiro, Grzybowski: Soviet Legal Institutions: Doctrines and Social Functions, 61 MICH. L. REV. 1382 (1963).

John L. Spivak. "Nazi Spies and American "Patriots." Souciant. http://souciant.com/2017/01/nazi-spies-and-american-patriots. Posted January 31, 2017.

"Just a Moment..." *Just a Moment..*, pitchbook.com/profiles/company/54689-95#overview. Accessed 2 Mar. 2024.

Kasparov, Garry. "Reading Russia: It's No Mystery". *Journal of Democracy*, vol. 20, no. 2, Apr. 2009, pp. 39-41.

Kenton, Will, and Robert C. Kelly. "What Is Nixon Shock? Definition, What Happened, and Aftereffects." *Investopedia*, 28 Feb. 2024, www.investopedia.com/terms/n/nixon-shock.asp. Accessed 10 Mar. 2024.

Kettle, Martin. "Nixon 'wrecked Early Peace in Vietnam'." *The Guardian*, 9 Aug. 2000, www.theguardian.com/world/2000/aug/09/martinkettle1. Accessed 10 Mar. 2024.

Kifner, John. "John Service, a Purged 'China Hand,' Dies at 89." *The New York Times - Breaking News, US News, World News and Videos*, 4 Feb. 1999, www.nytimes.com/1999/02/04/world/john-service-a-purged-china-hand-dies-at-89.html. Accessed 9 Mar. 2024.

Krauss, Charles. "Nixon's 1972 Visit to China at 50." *Wilson Center*, 21 Feb. 2022, www.wilsoncenter.org/blog-post/nixons-1972-visit-china-50. Accessed 10 Mar. 2024.

Kazin, Michael (29 October 1998). *The Populist Persuasion: An American History*. Cornell University Press. pp. 124–125. ISBN 0801485584.

Knox, Liam. "Challenges Compound for U.S. Branch Campuses in China." *Inside Higher Ed | Higher Education News, Events and Jobs*, 6 July 2023, www.insidehighered.com/news/global/us-colleges-world/2023/07/06/challenges-compound-us-branch-campuses-china. Accessed 11 Mar. 2024.

Kunov, Andrei, et al. *Putin's 'Party of Power' and the Declining Power of Parties: In Russia*. The Foreign Policy Centre, 2005.

Lewis, Nathan. "BRICS Making Good Progress On Their Golden Path." *Forbes*, 24 Jan. 2024, www.forbes.com/sites/nathanlewis/2024/01/24/brics-making-good-progress-on-their-golden-path/?sh=5bb827ee549b. Accessed 10 Mar. 2024.

"Liberal Club." *Duke University Libraries | Duke University Libraries*, library.duke.edu/research/student-activism/student-organizations/liberalclubprofile. Accessed 11 Mar. 2024.

London, Eric. "Democratic Socialists of America Confront Left-wing Opposition to Biden by Shifting Further to the Right." *Democratic Socialists of America confront left-wing opposition to Biden by shifting further to the right*, World Socialist Web Site, 21 Feb. 2022, www.wsws.org/en/articles/2022/02/22/dsam-f22.html. Accessed 11 Mar. 2024.

Lynch, Sarah. "Leonardo DiCaprio says Malaysian financier planned to donate to Obama's 2012 campaign." *Reuters.com*, 4 Apr. 2023, www.reuters.com/legal/leonardo-dicaprio-us-court-testify-fugees-rapper-trial-2023-04-03/. Accessed 11 Mar. 2024.

"MAO ASKED TO SEE ROOSEVELT IN 1945." *The New York Times - Breaking News, US News, World News and Videos*, 21 Sept. 1972,

Marx, Karl, and Friedrich Engels. The Communist Manifesto. Penguin Classics, 2002.

MATTHEWS, MERRILL. "Matthews: Bidenomics is Xinomics with American Characteristics." *The Hill*, 21 Nov. 2023, thehill.com/opinion/4321120-matthews-bidenomics-is-xinomics-with-american-characteristics/. Accessed 11 Mar. 2024.

www.nytimes.com/1972/09/21/archives/mao-asked-to-see-roosevelt-in-1945.html. Accessed 7 Mar. 2024.

Navasky, Victor. A Matter of Opinion. New York, NY: Macmillan Publishers, 2005. Print.

Nedopil, Christoph (2023): "Countries of the Belt and Road Initiative"; Shanghai, Green Finance & Development Center, FISF Fudan University, www.greenfdc.org

Oelsner, Lesley. "Hammer Enters Plea In Nixon Fund Case." *The New York Times - Breaking News, US News, World News and Videos*, 2 Oct. 1975, www.nytimes.com/1975/10/02/archives/hammer-enters-plea-in-nixon-fund-case-hammer-pleads-guilty-of.html. Accessed 10 Mar. 2024.

Paloaltostaff. (2015). Millennials increasingly moving away from religion. Paloaltoonline.com

Papa, Mihaela. "As BRICS Cooperation Accelerates, is It Time for the US to Develop a BRICS Policy?" *The Fletcher School: A Graduate School of International Affairs | The Fletcher School*, 18 Aug. 2023, fletcher.tufts.edu/news-events/news/brics-cooperation-accelerates-it-time-us-develop-brics-policy. Accessed 11 Mar. 2024.

"Peter Hopkins." *Big Think*, bigthink.com/people/peterhopkins/. Accessed 2 Mar. 2024.

Pipes, Richard. Communism: A History. Modern Library, 2003.

Pollitt, Katha, "Down for the Count", The Nation (December 16, 2000).

Pomfret, John, and Matt Pottinger. "Xi Jinping Says He Is Preparing China for War." *Foreign Affairs*, 2 Oct. 2023, www.foreignaffairs.com/united-states/xi-jinping-says-he-preparing-china-war. Accessed 5 Mar. 2024.

"President Nixon Arrives in Moscow for Historic Summit." *HISTORY*, 9 Feb. 2010, www.history.com/this-day-in-history/president-nixon-in-moscow. Accessed 10 Mar. 2024.

"Prime Minister Justin Trudeau Meets with Governor of California Gavin Newsom." *Prime Minister of Canada*, 15 Nov. 2023, www.pm.gc.ca/en/news/readouts/2023/11/15/prime-minister-justin-trudeau-meets-governor-california-gavin-newsom. Accessed 11 Mar. 2024.

Ratner, Paul. "39 Years Ago, a KGB Defector Chillingly Predicted Modern America." *Big Think*, 13 Jan. 2023, bigthink.com/the-present/yuri-bezmenov/. Accessed 2 Mar. 2024.

"Recognition of the Soviet Union, 1933." *Office of the Historian*, history.state.gov/milestones/1921–1936/ussr. Accessed 8 Mar. 2024.

"Remarks at the Signing of the Roosevelt Campobello International Park Agreement." *Welcome to The American Presidency Project | The American Presidency Project*, www.presidency.ucsb.edu/documents/remarks-the-signing-the-roosevelt-campobello-international-park-agreement. Accessed 8 Mar. 2024.

Ross, Sean. "Is the United States a Market Economy or a Mixed Economy?" *Investopedia,* 16 Dec. 2023, www.investopedia.com/ask/answers/031815/united-states-considered-market-economy-or-mixed-economy.asp. Accessed 7 Mar. 2024.

Roth, Samantha-Jo. "Republican Lawmakers Push for Greater Scrutiny of Chinese 'sister Cities' in US." *Washington Examiner - Political News and Conservative Analysis About Congress, the President, and the Federal Government,* 19 Apr. 2023, www.washingtonexaminer.com/news/1266420/republican-lawmakers-push-for-greater-scrutiny-of-chinese-sister-cities-in-us/. Accessed 11 Mar. 2024.

Rothbard, Murray N. "Nixonian Socialism." *Mises Institute,* 19 Mar. 2022, mises.org/mises-daily/nixonian-socialism. Accessed 10 Mar. 2024.

Rummel, R. J. *China's Bloody Century: Genocide and Mass Murder Since 1900.* Transaction Publishers, 2011.

"Russian Organized Criminal Activities in California." *Intelligence Resource Program, Federation of American Scientists,* irp.fas.org/world/para/docs/rusorg4.htm. Accessed 4 Mar. 2024.

Seidl, Mark. "The Lend-Lease Program, 1941-1945." *FDR Presidential Library & Museum,* www.fdrlibrary.org/lend-lease. Accessed 7 Mar. 2024.

"Select Committee Unveils Report on Illegal PRC-Tied Biolab in Reedley, CA with McCarthy & Costa." *Select Committee on the*

CCP, 16 Nov. 2023, selectcommitteeontheccp.house.gov/media/press-releases/select-committee-unveils-report-illegal-prc-tied-biolab-reedley-ca-mccarthy. Accessed 10 Mar. 2024.

"September, 1936." *FDR: Day by Day*, www.fdrlibrary.marist.edu/daybyday/resource/september-1936-7/.

Sharansky, N. (2008). Defending Identity. Annapolis, MD: Naval Institute Press.

Smith, Marion. "Communism and Religion Can't Coexist." *Wsj.com*, 29 Aug. 2019, www.wsj.com/articles/communism-and-religion-cant-coexist-11567120938. Accessed 2 Mar. 2024.

"Smith, Gerald Lyman Kenneth." *Encyclopedia of Arkansas*, 22 Sept. 2023, encyclopediaofarkansas.net/entries/gerald-lyman-kenneth-smith-1767/. Accessed 7 Mar. 2024.

"Strong's Hebrew: 7189. קֹשְׁטְ (qoshet) -- Truth." *Bible Hub: Search, Read, Study the Bible in Many Languages*, biblehub.com/hebrew/7189.htm. Accessed 2 Mar. 2024.

The Status of Anti-Communist Legislation, 1965 *Duke Law Journal* 369-385 (1965)

"THIRD PARTY TRIES WINGS IN CHICAGO; Newton Jenkins Is Entered for Mayor Under Symbol of the American Buffalo". *New York Times*. 27 January 1935. Retrieved 5 January 2019.

Tirone, Jonathan. "Why the US and Europe Still Buy Russian Nuclear Fuel." *The Washington Post*, 27 Aug. 2023, www.washingtonpost.com/business/energy/2023/08/27/why-the-us-and-europe-still-buy-russian-nuclear-fuel/23474ddc-44cd-11ee-b76b-0b6e5e92090d_story.html. Accessed 4 Mar. 2024.

Truitt, E.R. "Surveillance, Companionship, and Entertainment: The Ancient History of Intelligent Machines." *The MIT Press Reader*, 24 Nov. 2021, thereader.mitpress.mit.edu/the-ancient-history-of-intelligent-machines/. Accessed 12 Mar. 2024.

ReliefWeb, 30 June 2008, reliefweb.int/report/afghanistan/turning-afghan-heroin-kalashnikovs. Accessed 15 Mar. 2024.

"Understanding Circumstantial Evidence in Criminal Cases." Everett Gaskins Hancock LLP, www.egattorneys.com/circumstantial-evidence-in-criminal-cases. Accessed 3 Mar. 2024.

Van Der Toorn, K., Becking, B., & Van Der Horst, P. W. (1999). *Dictionary of deities and demons in the Bible (DDD)* (2nd ed.). William B. Eedermans Publishing Company.

Vickery, Matthew. "The Birthplace of the Illuminati." *BBC Breaking News, World News, U.S. News, Sports, Business, Innovation, Climate, Culture, Travel, Video & Audio*, 28 Nov. 2017, www.bbc.com/travel/article/20171127-the-birthplace-of-the-illuminati. Accessed 2 Mar. 2024.

WANG, Christoph N. "Countries of the Belt and Road Initiative (BRI)." *Green Finance & Development Center – Research, Advisory and Capacity Building for Greening Finance and Development*, greenfdc.org/countries-of-the-belt-and-road-initiative-bri/.

Wedel, Janine R. "Aid to Russia." *Institute for Policy Studies*, ips-dc.org/aid_to_russia/. Accessed 4 Mar. 2024.

Weir, Fred. "Putin's United Russia: Communist Party Clone or Modern Democratic Force?" *The Christian Science Monitor*, 4 Oct. 2011, www.csmonitor.com/World/Europe/2011/1004/Putin-s-United-Russia-Communist-Party-clone-or-modern-democratic-force. Accessed 4 Mar. 2024.

Weiss, Philip. "Kissinger '73: 'If They Put Jews in Gas Chambers in the Soviet Union, It's Not an American Concern'." *Mondoweiss*, 11 Dec. 2010, mondoweiss.net/2010/12/kissinger-73-if-they-put-jews-in-gas-chambers-in-the-soviet-union-its-not-an-american-concern/. Accessed 10 Mar. 2024.

"What Does 'path of Socialism with Chinese Characteristics' Mean?" *CGTN | Breaking News, China News, World News and Video*, www.cgtn.com/how-china-works/feature/What-does-path-of-socialism-with-Chinese-characteristics-mean.html. Accessed 3 Mar. 2024.

"What is Most Significant in the Pentagon's China Military Report?" *Reuters*, 21 Oct. 2023, www.reuters.com/world/what-is-most-significant-pentagons-china-military-report-2023-10-21/. Accessed 5 Mar. 2024.

"Which Countries Are Communist?" *Encyclopedia Britannica,* www.britannica.com/question/Which-countries-are-communist. Accessed 3 Mar. 2024.

"Whipping Stagflation - Digital History." *University of Houston,* www.digitalhistory.uh.edu/disp_textbook.cfm.   Accessed 10 Mar. 2024.

Wong, Chun H. "China's Xi Is Resurrecting Mao's 'Continuous Revolution' With a Twist." *Wsj.com,* 1 Jan. 2024, www.wsj.com/world/china/chinas-xi-is-resurrecting-maos-continuous-revolution-with-a-twist-ed5ec610.   Accessed 6 Mar. 2024.

"World War II Allies: U.S. Lend-Lease to the Soviet Union, 1941-1945." *U.S. Embassy and Consulates in Russia,* ru.usembassy.gov/world-war-ii-allies-u-s-lend-lease-to-the-Soviet-union-1941
1945/

"The National Recovery Administration and the Schechter Brothers." *Bill of Rights Institute,* billofrightsinstitute.org/essays/the-national-recovery-administration-and-the-schechter-brothers.   Accessed 7 Mar. 2024.

NEUMEISTER, LARRY, and ERIC TUCKER. "Secret Chinese Police Station in New York Leads to Arrests." *AP News,* 17 Apr. 2023, apnews.com/article/chinese-government-justice-department-new-york-police-transnational-repression-05624126f8e6cb00cf9ae3cb01767fa1.   Accessed 11 Mar. 2024.

"The   World   in   2050."   *PwC*,   Feb.   2017, www.pwc.com/gx/en/research-insights/economy/the-world-in-2050.html. Accessed 6 Mar. 2024.